JONATHAN EDWARDS

JONATHAN EDWARDS

Puritan, Preacher, Philosopher

John E. Smith

UNIVERSITY OF NOTRE DAME PRESS

First published in 1992 by
Geoffrey Chapman
Villiers House, 41/47 Strand
London WC2N 5JE
and in the USA by
University of Notre Dame Press
Notre Dame, Indiana 46556

Manufactured in the United Kingdom

First published 1992

Library of Congress Cataloging-in-Publication Data

Smith, John E.
Jonathan Edwards : puritan, preacher, philosopher / John E. Smith.
p. cm. — (Outstanding Christian thinkers)
Includes index.
ISBN 0-268-01192-3
1. Edwards, Jonathan, 1703–1758. I. Title.
II. Series.
BX7280.E3S57 1992
15.8′092—dc20 92-37017
[B] CIP

Front cover: portrait of Reverend Jonathan Edwards by Joseph Badger, reproduced by kind permission of the Yale University Art Gallery, bequest of Eugene Phelps Edwards
Photograph of author: Yale University, Office of Public Information

Typeset by Colset Private Limited, Singapore
Printed and bound in Great Britain by
Biddles Ltd, Guildford and King's Lynn

Editorial foreword

St Anselm of Canterbury once described himself as someone with faith seeking understanding. In words addressed to God he says 'I long to understand in some degree thy truth, which my heart believes and loves. For I do not seek to understand that I may believe, but I believe in order to understand.'

And this is what Christians have always inevitably said, either explicitly or implicitly. Christianity rests on faith, but it also has content. It teaches and proclaims a distinctive and challenging view of reality. It naturally encourages reflection. It is something to think about, something about which one might even have second thoughts.

But what have the greatest Christian thinkers said? And is it worth saying? Does it engage with modern problems? Does it provide us with a vision to live by? Does it make sense? Can it be preached? Is it believable?

The subject of the present volume, the Calvinist theologian Jonathan Edwards, was a vigorous and influential force in the history of Christianity in New England. The target of much hostility and disparagement in his lifetime, Edwards has since come to be rated as the most significant of American Puritan theologians and as the most astute American philosopher up to the time of Charles Peirce (1839–1914). He was also a renowned preacher, apologist and historian. There are reasons for describing him as America's greatest religious thinker.

As well as providing biographical material on Edwards, Professor Smith deals with all the major aspects of his teaching. He especially aims at highlighting Edwards's ability as a philosopher and philosophical theologian. The achievements of Edwards scholars since 1949, together with the Editors' Introductions to the definitive Yale edition of Edwards's *Works*, have enabled Professor Smith to write about Edwards in a new way. They have helped him to offer a more

Contents

Preface

I would like to pay tribute to the memory of Perry Miller of Harvard University who, more than thirty years ago, first had the vision of a critical edition of the writings of Jonathan Edwards, based on both previously printed first editions and the large body of hitherto unpublished manuscripts in the Beinecke Rare Book and Manuscript Library at Yale University and in the Library of the Andover-Newton Theological Seminary. The result was the initiation of *The Works of Jonathan Edwards*, published by Yale University Press (1957–), in which the next forthcoming volume, 10, will be the first one in the series of *Sermons*. I am much indebted to Miller's work concerning Edwards and the Puritan tradition he inherited. I would also like to express profound appreciation for the devoted work of the editors of each volume and for the advice and assistance of the Editorial Committee over so long a time. No one can encompass the whole of Edwards's thought with equal depth and understanding, and therefore I am pleased to acknowledge how much I have learned from the scholars whose work I cite in the following pages. The interpretations are, of course, my own and I bear the sole responsibility for them.

I also wish to express gratitude to Mrs Alan Slatter who so painstakingly typed the manuscript, which is no mean task in view of Edwards's often unusual constructions, punctuation and the use of expressions like ''em' for 'them', and many others.

John E. Smith
New Haven, Connecticut

informed look at Edwards's relation to the thought of John Locke (1632–1704) than has hitherto been available. They have helped him to deal with the full scope of Edwards's *Ethical Writings*. They have also helped him to emphasize Edwards's perceptive work as a historian, both sacred and secular, in his remarkable series of sermons known as *A History of the Work of Redemption*.

Professor Smith is uniquely qualified to introduce readers to the thinking of Jonathan Edwards. A much esteemed figure on the landscape of modern American philosophical theology, he has been General Editor of the Yale edition of Edwards's writings since 1963. His book is the first to take advantage of all the new material which has emerged in the production of this first critical editing of Edwards's writings.

Brian Davies OP

Short titles for works cited

In Edwards's time the titles of most books were long because they were designed to describe a topic and sometimes the thesis to be attacked or defended. Edwards's titles are no exception. For the sake of brevity, a short title will be used for each work cited with the exception of the *Personal Narrative*.

Charity	*Charity and its Fruits*
Distinguishing Marks	*The Distinguishing Marks of a Work of the Spirit of God*
'Divine Light'	'A Divine and Supernatural Light'
End of Creation	*Concerning the End for which God Created the World*
Faithful Narrative	*A Faithful Narrative of the Surprising Work of God*
Freedom of the Will	*A Careful and Strict Inquiry into . . . Freedom of the Will*
History of Redemption	*A History of the Work of Redemption*
'God Glorified'	'God Glorified in the Work of Redemption' (also known as 'God Glorified in Man's Dependence')
Original Sin	*The Great Christian Doctrine of Original Sin Defended*
Religious Affections	*A Treatise Concerning Religious Affections*
'Sinners'	'Sinners in the Hands of an Angry God'

JONATHAN EDWARDS

Some Thoughts	*Some Thoughts Concerning the Present Revival of Religion in New England*
True Virtue	*On the Nature of True Virtue*

1

Jonathan Edwards: his life and times

Edwards was unquestionably the major theologian of American Puritanism; he was also the most acute philosophical thinker on the American scene up to the time of Charles Peirce. The two thinkers have something significant in common: the ability to reshape ideas inherited from abroad in the light of the needs and interests of the American situation. Edwards drew inspiration from Locke's empiricism and, under the guidance of his own experience and the events of the revivals, revamped it by bringing understanding, will and affections into a new unity, and by stressing the continuity and cumulative character of experience as the very substance of a person's life. Peirce acknowledged his indebtedness to Kant, Duns Scotus and a number of other thinkers and went on to develop a new categorial scheme that owed something to Kant, but more to the new emphasis on evolutionary growth, real possibilities and the belief so integral a part of life in America, that ideas are not inert but express the dynamism of things and of human behaviour. Both, moreover, saw the importance of *practice*—of the upshot of human beliefs and propensities—and neither allowed the reasonableness, the understanding implicit in purposeful conduct to be obscured by simple oppositions between 'theory' and 'practice'. Edwards and Peirce benefited from the thought of others, but were not limited by it; each thought for himself in the light of his own experience and the demands of the times in which he lived.

Unlike an Immanuel Kant whose life throws little light on the intricacies of his thought, Edwards's life was closely intertwined with the doctrines of his treatises and the rhetoric of his sermons. So much of his writing and his preaching was in response to the events that shaped his age; the need he saw to defend the basic Calvinist tradition against the

Arminians, the overpowering phenomenon of the Great Awakening; his struggles with the Williamses, and his final confrontation with the congregation at Northampton. And yet Edwards always seemed a man apart, someone whose intellect was beyond the reach of the ordinary church member and whose vision extended to the whole of human history so that being hidden away in Northampton seemed to be a merely accidental fact about his being. As the record shows, however, he was more intimately involved with his congregation than might be supposed, although he devoted a great portion of his time to writing in his study. Perry Miller is right in his claim that the real life of Edwards was the life of the mind and Edwards's many writings substantiate that claim. But we cannot ignore the fact that Edwards was involved in just about every controversy that raged in his time and therefore we cannot afford to lose sight of the events that were often the occasion for his thought. Miller, with a very considerable success, dealt with the problem by proposing an 'external' and an 'internal' biography of Edwards which he narrated alternately in an attempt to show the integration between the two.[1]

Few students of Edwards's work have failed to take note of the many facets of the man. He was an *exegetical preacher* who took this task very seriously, as is shown by the body of sermons that have survived. There exist in manuscript some six hundred written-out sermons in little booklets which Edwards prepared himself. In addition, there are many sermon outlines among his manuscripts, since after 1741 he no longer wrote out his sermons fully, but used only key words and supplied biblical passages from memory. He was a *polemicist* to be reckoned with, as we see in *Original Sin*, a relentless attack on John Taylor's (1694–1761) *Scripture-Doctrine of Original Sin* (1740), in *Freedom of the Will*, where he engaged no less than three Arminian opponents—Daniel Whitby (1638–1726), Thomas Chubb (1679–1747), and Isaac Watts (1674–1748)—and in a number of writings dealing with church polity. He was an *apologist* on behalf of Reformed doctrine, a role Edwards played throughout his writings. He was a *philosopher*, a metaphysician engaged with the question of Being as is evident from his 'Notes on the Mind', *True Virtue, End of Creation* and in many entries from the as yet unpublished *Miscellanies*. And that is not all; Edwards was also a *sacred historian*, especially in his *History of Redemption* where he outlined the full scope of the divine Providence from the Creation to the Last Judgement. The interesting fact is that, while all these facets were clearly interconnected in Edwards's mind, a reader concentrating on any one of them may well find the others falling from sight. One can read pages in his theological works without being particularly aware of Edwards the student of Locke and Isaac Newton (1642–1727) who had distinctive views of his own about ideas, the nature of the mind, the being of nature and the make-up of the human self.

Edwards was born on 5 October 1703 in East Windsor, Connecticut, the fifth child of Timothy and Esther Edwards in a family of eleven children. Timothy Edwards had been ordained minister in the east parish of Windsor in 1694; his wife, Esther, was a daughter of the Rev. Solomon Stoddard (1643–1729) of Northampton, Massachusetts. That relationship was to become highly important because Edwards became Stoddard's protégé even before he was called to be Stoddard's assistant in the church at Northampton, and Edwards was thus identified with the powers of the Connecticut valley in the contest with the Mathers who reigned in Boston. Stoddard was acutely aware of this rivalry and, although he was widely known for his power—he was openly referred to as the 'Pope' of the region—he was happy to have young Edwards at his side.

After receiving elementary schooling from his father—most ministers at the time ran a school along with their regular duties—in 1716 Edwards entered the Collegiate School, which was designated as Yale College two years later. Dispute about the location of the School went on for several years and in that time Edwards attended classes in Wethersfield, where he read Locke and Newton and began his 'Notes on the Mind' and 'Notes on Natural Science'. Edwards completed his studies in 1720 and two years later accepted a call to a Scotch Presbyterian church in New York. This move suggests not only Edwards's indifference to the forms of ecclesiastical polity, but also the cordial relations that held between Congregationalists and Presbyterians at the time.

His New York pastorate was not unsuccessful—he delivered some fine sermons there—but the church was not doing very well and in 1723 he accepted a call to a church in Bolton, Connecticut. This move was interrupted by an offer from Yale College and in 1724, having already completed his Master of Arts degree, he became senior tutor at Yale. The future, largely in the form of Stoddard, had a further call upon him. In 1725, the church in Northampton decided to find someone who could be Stoddard's successor and, finding Edwards eminently qualified, the congregation selected him. He was ordained in 1727 and later in the year married Sarah Pierrepont about whom he had already written a panegyric—'They say there is a young lady in [New Haven] who is beloved of that Great Being . . .'.

The next significant event in Edwards's life took place in July 1731, when he was invited to give the Public Lecture in Boston, the domain of Increase Mather (1639–1723) and his son Cotton Mather (1663–1728). This 'Thursday' lecture had long been established as an opportunity to hear all ministers preach and on this occasion it was Edwards's turn. As a rule, this lecture was less a sermon than a short treatise with theological content uppermost in importance. Edwards delivered the discourse that is generally known by its short title, 'God Glorified in Man's Dependence', and in it Edwards made no reference whatever to the 'Federal' theology based on the idea of a divine covenant, a theology dear to the hearts of most of the audience. This was a bold move indeed; Edwards could not have been unaware that he was on trial—a man from Yale and the Connecticut valley, and the heir of Stoddard as well, delivering what was essentially a challenge to the men of Harvard and of Boston, and in their own precincts. The Covenant theology had its roots in English Puritanism and *The Marrow of Puritan Divinity* of William Ames, the leading expositor of the covenant doctrine, was a second Bible to the ministers of New England.[2] Sydney Ahlstrom has given a brief and lucid statement of what was at issue:

> The heart of covenant theology was the insistence that God's predestinating decrees were not part of a vast impersonal and mechanical scheme, but that, under the Gospel dispensation, God had established a covenant of grace with the seed of Abraham. This was to be appropriated in faith, and hence was irreducibly personal. Puritans disagreed as to how much was God's work, and how much preparation for grace the natural man could do, but they tended to agree that the effectual call of each elect saint of God would always come as an individuated encounter with God's promises. One would then make a covenant with God, as had Abraham of old.[3]

Edwards would have none of this doctrine; his rejection of it was implied in his ignoring the whole idea. Instead he insisted at the outset on an uncompromising and total dependence of man on God and declared that this very dependence manifests the true *gloria* of God. 'There is', he wrote, 'an absolute and universal dependence of the redeemed on God. The nature and contrivances of our redemption is such, that the redeemed are in every thing directly, immediately, and entirely dependent on God: They are dependent on him for all, and are dependent on him every way.'[4] Edwards went on to develop this doctrine, showing that God is the *first cause* of all the good the redeemed enjoy, the only source of grace, and that all who are called and sanctified 'are to attribute it alone to the good pleasure of God's goodness'. The only reference Edwards made to a *covenant* was to point out that before the Fall—'under the first covenant'—we depended entirely on God's goodness, but that in our present state 'we are now more dependent on God's arbitrary and sovereign good pleasure . . . than under the first covenant'. The message was clear; Edwards was reaffirming the Calvinist heritage and the belief that there are no limits to God's power and that no human conditions can be attached to his sovereign grace. The idea of a covenant seemed to Edwards as a 'mediating' element that came between the judgement of God and the individual, as if God were somehow bound to show mercy to those who had made a covenant with him. This belief was central to Edwards's entire theology and it was to be the cornerstone of the *Freedom of the Will* in which he argued that if there is any self-determining initiative in the human will, God is excluded from the universe. In philosophical terms, there are no secondary causes; all causation flows from the one source of power in the universe. We shall have occasion to consider later on whether this view is consistent with Edwards's belief that God is related to the creatures in ways appropriate to their particular natures. If so, how is the one cause doctrine able to allow for the differences between stars, animals and human beings?

In 1734 Edwards's preaching was making its impact and it sparked a revival that lasted until the end of the following year. He reported a 'great many surprising conversions' two of which were to figure in one of the most powerful books Edwards ever wrote, *A Faithful Narrative of the Surprising Work of God in the Conversion of Many Hundred Souls in Northampton, and the Neighboring Towns and Villages.* This work was published in 1736 and went through three editions and twenty printings by 1739. According to Miller (p. 137), it was still a 'handbook of revivalism' a hundred years later.

The chief appeal of the book was its vivid portrayal of individual experience or what Edwards called 'experiential religion'. Edwards chose to describe the religious quest of two very different persons: Abigail Hutchinson, a frail, unmarried woman who died prematurely, and Phebe Bartlett, a child of four who was extraordinary in her concern for the things of religion. Abigail, says Edwards, was a 'still, quiet, reserved person' and he was careful to point out that 'there was nothing in her education that tended to *enthusiasm*'.[5] 'She was first awakened', Edwards writes, 'in the winter season . . . by something she heard her brother say of the necessity of being in good earnest in seeking regenerating grace.' Her great terror was that she had sinned against God and she confessed that she had 'trusted to her own prayers and religious performances' but to no avail; she resolved to go to the minister for help. Gradually her life was turned around. 'She had', Edwards writes, 'many extraordinary discoveries of the glory of God and Christ' and 'Once, when she came to me, she said, that at such and such a time, she thought she saw as much of God and had as much joy and pleasure, as was possible in this life . . .'. Abigail told Edwards as well that after her apprehension of God's glory, 'She saw the same things as before, yet more clearly, and in a far more excellent and delightful manner'. If this observation was Abigail's own memory of what happened to her, and not an interpolation by Edwards, it is a matter of considerable importance. Edwards had insisted in 'A Divine and Supernatural Light' (1734) that spiritual understanding does not mean the coming of new ideas or doctrines, but is instead a new perception, a new sense of the excellency and beauty of what we apprehended before. He was to stress the same point later on in *Religious Affections* (1746).

The story of Phebe's experience was told to Edwards by her parents, 'whose veracity none who know them doubt of'. The young child was much given to praying alone in her closet and on one occasion told her mother that she was unsuccessful in her quest for God and said, 'I am afraid that I shall go to hell!' after which she continued crying and talking, but could not be consoled. 'Till at length', Edwards writes, 'she suddenly ceased crying, and began to smile, and presently said with a smiling countenance, Mother, the kingdom of heaven has come to me!' 'From this time', Edwards reports, 'there appeared a very remarkable abiding change in the child.'

The chief significance in Edwards's *Personal Narrative* is that it shows the empirical attitude at work. In these two studies, he was describing and interpreting actual experience as a way of looking into the heart of the activity of the Spirit in regeneration. He was not engaged in theological accounts of the manner in which the transformation is *supposed to* take place, but instead in the description of what *actually* happened to Abigail and Phebe. One of Edwards's important departures from the tradition was his rejection of the widespread belief that regeneration follows a standard pattern or order in the soul and that this order is a reliable criterion for judging the state of a person. Instead Edwards laid great stress in the *Personal Narrative* on the idea that the 'manner' of conversion is 'various' and dependent on many different factors, including the temperament of individuals. Edwards was striking the note that William James was to sound many years later when he wrote about the 'varieties of religious experience'. As we will see, this matter was of the utmost importance to Edwards when he came to develop his conception of 'signs' manifest in gracious affections. There he insisted that the *intrinsic nature* of these affections is the significant fact about them and the *order* in which they appear is wholly beside the point. As he was fond of saying, the Bible speaks much about the fruits of the Spirit (what he called 'affections'), but nowhere does it speak about the manner or the order in which the Spirit brings them about.

Another idea of no less importance stands out in Edwards's *Personal*

Narrative: grace comes neither from reasonable persuasion nor from some physical influx, but is instead a matter of perception or a form of apprehension. The fundamental change in the person has mainly to do with a new foundation in the soul which Edwards repeatedly described in aesthetic terms as the beauty of holiness, the delight experienced in grasping what he called the 'excellency' of God, Christ, the Bible and all the fruits of the Spirit.[6] Once again the originality of Edwards shines through; he was forever seeking to go beyond the old dichotomies and alternatives that had divided Puritan thought from the outset and to suggest, in the arresting idea of Wittgenstein, 'possibilities that you had not thought of'. The strength of Edwards's position is that he could point to experience as he knew it in support of his ideas and not have to depend on previous authorities. Edwards had not read Locke and Newton for nothing, and indeed he was prompted by their general outlook to insist that all religious experience should find concrete expression in words. He may have been too sanguine in his belief that if the person does not have the ability to capture the meaning of his or her experience in language, there is no grace present at all. This ability he regarded as a *test*, the linchpin of empiricism, and it points ahead to the emphasis he was to place on the importance of signs in the life and conduct of the person as indications of the presence of the Spirit.

The next chapter in the odyssey of Edwards was undoubtedly the revivals of 1740, far more widespread and intense than any of the preceding stirrings; it was this revival that came to be known to New England Puritanism as the Great Awakening. While this phenomenon had profound repercussions on the American scene for both religion and the society at large, it should be seen alongside of its parallels in Europe. There was Pietism in Germany and the founding of Methodism through the work of the Wesleys in England; despite important differences, these movements shared a common core—a concern for individual experience and the engagement of the heart which seemed to have been subordinated through either the domination of doctrine or the emphasis placed on liturgy in the Churches.[7] A typical stereotype of Protestantism is that it is passionate, 'evangelical', and an expression of individual feeling in contrast to the imposing philosophical theologies of the great Doctors of the Roman Catholic Church in the Middle Ages. The truth is that, having denied the authority of the Pope and the *magisterium*, the Reformed Churches stood in need of a new source of unity and authority. The result was the appeal to the Bible, to Creeds and Confessions and to new systems of theology as means of establishing unity and identity among the Reformed Churches. In short, contrary to popular conceptions, Protestantism became quite rationalistic in the centuries after Luther and adherence to authoritative theologies and ecclesiastical canons became mandatory. The reaction to this state of affairs, not unlike the reaction of Romanticism to the rationalism of the Enlightenment in Europe, took the form of a new appeal to individual experience, to feeling and to what Edwards called 'heart' religion.

The Awakening of 1740–41 was the culmination of a long series of revivalistic efforts. As early as 1719, Theodore Frelinghuysen, a pastor in the Dutch Reformed Church, led revival meetings in New Jersey, and William Tennent (1673–1745) established the Log College (1736) in Pennsylvania. This College became a model for schools seeking to combine learning with evangelical fervour. The Awakening, moreover, continued to have effects on education long after it died out in New England. Jonathan Dickinson was led to found the College of New Jersey (later Princeton University) in 1746. Anglicans and conservative Presbyterians cooperated in the founding of King's College (later Columbia University) in 1754, evangelical Baptists lent their support to the College of Rhode Island (later Brown University) in 1764, and Dutch Reformed revivalists founded Queen's College (later Rutgers, and even later the University of New Jersey) in 1766. This concern for education among the Protestant churches was something of great importance and Edwards focused that concern by his insistence on the need for an educated ministry in opposition to the evangelical anti-intellectual tendency to set 'having the spirit' against all forms of 'book learning'.

Although Edwards's preaching and writing were major factors in bringing on the Awakening, we must not overlook the powerful opposition he had to contend with. His most formidable opponent by far was Charles Chauncy (1705–87), a graduate of Harvard and the pastor of the First Church in Boston for half a century. Chauncy, moreover, had allies in his campaign against revivalism in the form of three influential ministers—the Whittelseys—Samuel (1686–1752) and his two sons, Samuel, Jr (1713–68) and Chauncey (1717–87). No one of these supporters was up to the level of Charles Chauncy who, though a dull preacher, was regarded as a man of great learning. Chauncy, in turn, was no match for Edwards whose subtleties he invariably missed and, while what Chauncy represented prevailed over Edwards at the time, Edwards's stature has continued to grow and Chauncy's name is known only to historians.

It would, however, be a great mistake to suppose that the situation was simply a struggle between two individuals defending two opposed viewpoints about the nature of true piety. Things were more intricate than that as we can see from the fact that Edwards was cast in the role of mediator, a position in which he was open to attack from partisans of both extremes. If we consider that at one extreme there stood a rationalism represented by Chauncy and totally opposed to the uncontrolled emotionalism and enthusiasm represented by a James Davenport at the other pole, it becomes clear that Edwards did not fit into either camp. He was certainly a defender of the revivals and of experiential religion and thus in general disagreement with Chauncy. He was, however, determined not only to disassociate himself from James Davenport's wild ravings, but also to prevent Chauncy and his followers from identifying heart religion with the excesses that made it easy for them to condemn revivalism out of hand. Edwards was in a position of extreme difficulty; on the one hand he believed in the validity of a religion of the heart against the rationalists and their more 'decorous' piety and hence he drew their fire; on the other hand, he demanded that heart religion—the religious affections—be subjected to tests in order to assess their validity and this demand set him at odds with the revivalists who claimed immediate certainty about their spiritual state and hence thought that critical judgement was beside the point. Edwards was to provide a brilliant, but quite subtle, theory that sought to do some justice to both sides in his *Religious Affections* of 1746 and, although it arrived too late on the scene to figure in the actual controversy, that work still stands as one of the best analyses of experience in religion ever written.

Let us, however, go back to Chauncy and Davenport in order to draw the picture more clearly. James Davenport (1716–57) represented what was worst in the whole revival picture and it is generally agreed that, in comparison with his behaviour, George Whitefield (1714–70) and Tennent were 'models of decorum'. Davenport was a great-grandson of John Davenport (1597–1670), the founder of New Haven, and minister of the old Puritan church in Southold on Long Island. In 1741 he was determined to follow in the footsteps of Whitefield and Tennent and set out to become one of the most powerful awakeners. He was clearly a fanatic and somewhat unstable; he did not hesitate to confront ministers of the time—including Chauncy himself—and demand to know whether or not they were converted. He ran afoul of Connecticut's law against itinerant preachers and was deported under guard to Long Island. After a futile attempt to set up a separatist church in New London, Davenport was persuaded by two ministers to repent, which he did by publishing *Confessions and Retractions* in 1744.

Chauncy, as may easily be imagined, identified revivalism—'religious commotions'—with the behaviour of Davenport and the preaching of Whitefield and Tennent. As Miller (p. 172) nicely expresses the point, 'To our reading, Davenport was insane, but to Chauncy he was only slightly more so than Whitefield and Tennent'. In 1741 Edwards published, under the title of *The Distinguishing Marks of a Work of the Spirit of God*, several sermons he had delivered at New Haven. The stage was now set for the debate between Edwards and Chauncy. In the *Distinguishing Marks*, a forerunner of the *Religious Affections* to come, Edwards cited five 'marks' which he later called 'signs' through which to discern the presence of the Spirit.

Edwards was clearly issuing a challenge to Chauncy, although he does not mention his name. What is most significant in this work is that Edwards set forth a list of natural and social phenomena—shrieking and writhing, the having of visions, vain imaginings, and the like—which, he argued, would necessarily accompany *any* upheaval or departure from the normal state of affairs. Edwards, moreover, admitted that these phenomena could be explained in psychological terms 'from what we know of the nature of man' and provide no basis whatever for judging the validity of religious revivalism. Edwards's contention is that it is 'natural' to the human constitution to cry out in joy or to groan under the weight of anguish—'If people are affected, can they be kept from making noises?' He anticipated that Chauncy's response would take the form of a natural or sociological analysis of the revival issuing in the conclusion that there was nothing divine in it at all. In claiming that the *excesses* and 'natural' accompaniments manifested in the revivals—what he later referred to as the 'tares' that inevitably grow along with wheat—are inessential, Edwards was attempting to defuse any arguments against the revival based chiefly on these side-effects.

In 1743 Chauncy published *The Late Religious Commotions in New England Considered* which was a reply to Edwards's New Haven sermon. The main thrust of his argument is that no solid evidence of the presence of the Spirit has been given and that what happened in the revivals could be explained as natural effects of overwrought passions. This line of thought is typical of Chauncy's approach; reason and judgement are set on one side and over against them are imagination and emotion. God speaks to us through reason, while Satan works through imagination and the passions and in this way deludes both. Although Edwards could not accept this oversimplified picture, the reference to what Satan can do troubled him so much that later on in *Religious Affections* he made a point not only of attacking Chauncy's head/heart dichotomy, but also of showing what Satan *cannot* do.[8]

In 1742 Edwards published *Some Thoughts Concerning the Present Revival of Religion in New England* in which he claimed that the revival was 'in general and on the whole' a true work of the Spirit. Chauncy, however, had yet another weapon in his arsenal and it took the form of a book, *Seasonal Thoughts on the State of Religion in New England* (1743), which Miller (p. 175) has described as 'a massive, Johnsonian, indignant work, a source book for American communal behavior; learned and dignified, it is monumentally honest'. In preparation for this book, Chauncy took Edwards's advice to his opponents to observe the evidence for themselves, and Chauncy did just that. The following is an account of what he witnessed:

> The Meeting was carried on with what seemed to me great Confusion; some screaming out in distress and Anguish; some praying; others singing; some again jumping up and down the House, while others were exhorting; some lying along on the Floor, and others walking and talking: The whole was a very great Noise, to be heard at a Mile's distance, and continued almost the whole Night. (Miller, p. 175)

Chauncy was, of course, focusing attention on just those features of religious revivalism which Edwards was so bent on declaring to be inessential because, in his view, they prove nothing. Chauncy saw things otherwise; for him an enlightened mind should be our guide, not raised affections. The point was not lost on Edwards and in *Religious Affections* he sought to deal with the problem, first, with the concept of affections itself—affections are a synthesis of *idea* and *sense*, understanding and will—and, second, by insisting that true affections 'are not all heat and no light'.

The next years of Edwards's life were marked by a worsening of his relations with his church and the town, and his melancholy over the end of the Awakening. He wrote to one of his several correspondents in Scotland lamenting the fact that the Awakening was dead. Trouble was brewing in the congregation; a number of children were found reading a 'bad book'—a manual for midwives—and among them were the offspring of influential people who did not look at all kindly on Edwards for conducting an interrogation of the culprits and demanding a public confession. And this was not all; the tension was mounting over Edwards's insistence on a public profession of faith as a condition for church membership, especially since this stance was taken as a sign that he was not carrying on Stoddard's tradition of admitting candidates without such a profession. The matter did not come to a head until some years later because of the ironic fact that no candidates presented themselves after 1744, some six years before Edwards was to be dismissed in 1750. This state of affairs could well have been the basis for the congregation's belief that no one could pass the test that Edwards would impose.[9]

In 1749 Edwards made fully explicit his view about church membership in a work with a very long title which is best known in its abbreviated form, *Qualifications for Communion.*[10] Now there was no more doubt about his defection from Stoddard nor about his intention to demand public profession. The controversy was by no means purely theological; many other factors were involved in virtue of the intermingling of the affairs of church and town. Edwards's opponents, not only among the ministers but among the real estate and business interests as well, succeeded in bringing the dispute under the jurisdiction of a precinct committee—the state would be heard as well as the church—and in the end Edwards was defeated. By a margin of one vote it was recommended that he and the church at Northampton should be separated; in 1750 Edwards delivered his 'Farewell Sermon'.

In the following year Edwards was advised to accept a call that he had received from the church at Stockbridge several months after his dismissal from Northampton. In Stockbridge he preached to the Indians, endured the hardships of being on the edge of the French and Indian Wars begun in 1754, published *Freedom of the Will* in the same year, and *Original Sin* in 1758. After the death in 1757 of Aaron Burr who had been President of the College of New Jersey, the Trustees invited Edwards to be his successor. After writing a long letter in which he set down what he regarded as his *dis*qualifications for the post, Edwards accepted the call. His arrival in Princeton in 1758 coincided with an epidemic of smallpox; he was vaccinated against the disease but died within less than four weeks. The man who began his relations with academic life as tutor at Yale thus ended them as President of Princeton; a remarkable odyssey.

Notes

1 Since we cannot recount Edwards's biography in detail readers are referred to Perry Miller's *Jonathan Edwards* (New York: William Sloane Associates, 1949), to Ola Elizabeth Winslow, *Jonathan Edwards 1703–1758: A Biography* (New York: Macmillan, 1940), and to the 'Life of President Edwards' by Sereno Edwards Dwight, included in his edition of Edwards's *Works* (1830).

2 William Ames (1576–1633), *Medulla Sacrae Theologiae* (1623), trans. as *The Marrow of Sacred Divinity* (1642).

3 Sydney E. Ahlstrom, *A Religious History of the American People* (New Haven and London: Yale University Press, 1972), p. 131.

4 The passage quoted is the opening sentence of the sermon, 'God Glorified in Man's Dependence'. The full text is to be found in *Jonathan Edwards, Representative Selections*, ed. Clarence H. Faust and Thomas H. Johnson (New York: American Book Company, 1935), pp. 92–101.

5 *Enthusiasm* (literally, 'being filled with the god' or 'being inspired') was the word used to describe belief in private revelations from God in which

the meaning of some particular biblical text was disclosed to a person. Edwards was much opposed to this idea; revelation is completed in the Bible and no new revelations are to be countenanced.

6 The best account that has been given of the aesthetic dimension in Edwards's thought is found in Roland A. Delattre, *Beauty and Sensibility in the Thought of Jonathan Edwards* (New Haven and London: Yale University Press, 1968).

7 John Wesley was greatly impressed by Edwards's *Narrative*, as was the English evangelist, George Whitefield, who read the work when he was preaching in Georgia in 1738. Between that date and 1770 Whitefield was to make no less than seven trips to America, preaching revival sermons from south to north. He was a sensational speaker and not all pulpits were open to him, but Edwards invited him to preach at Northampton. Although Edwards could say that Whitefield left the whole society 'sweetly melted', he had reservations on two counts. Edwards was uneasy about Whitefield's encouragement of enthusiasm, and he disapproved of Whitefield's view—popular among itinerant evangelists who had no congregations of their own—that the people should abandon 'unconverted ministers'. Since most evangelists thought of themselves as converted, they were greatly tempted to pass adverse judgement on the spiritual state of ministers in settled churches. Edwards regarded this as divisive and even as irresponsible, since it was quite easy for itinerants to move into a town, 'revive' the people, and then be gone without a thought of the situation they left behind.

8 We shall postpone detailed discussion of this and related points until Chapter 3, in which the main focus will be *Religious Affections*. In that work Edwards incorporated the ideas in all of his previous revival writings and went beyond them through the conceptions of affections, the sense of the heart and what he called spiritual understanding.

9 Edwards seems never to have considered the inherent contradiction between his claim that the signs of gracious affections are meant exclusively for individual self-examination and his call for a public profession of faith. He repeatedly insisted that no one is to apply these signs in judgement of the state of any other; God alone is the judge. Unless, however, the confession by an individual is accepted *without question* by the minister and senior members of the congregation, any *appraisal* of its genuineness must constitute a case of some person or persons judging the spiritual state of another person. The problem here is not the issue of whether profession is required or not, but the conditions under which any profession is to be considered.

It may be, however, that Edwards did have some inkling of the problem in the great emphasis he placed in *Religious Affections* on the twelfth sign, which is *holy practice*. Conduct is open and public, even if the 'heart' it expresses is not. Any judgement about the *behaviour* of another might be construed as a public matter and not as an effort to judge the 'sincerity' of the person. The issue is discussed at some length by David Hall in his Introduction to the *Ecclesiastical Writings* to be published later in the Yale edition of *The Works of Jonathan Edwards*.

10 *An Humble Inquiry into The Rules of the Word of God Concerning Qualifications Requisite to a Compleat Standing and Full Communion in the Visible Christian Church* (1749).

2

Edwards's thought and the philosophy of Locke

It is quite clear that Edwards found great inspiration in Locke's celebrated *Essay Concerning Human Understanding* (first published 1690), and there can be no doubt that Locke's appeal to experience had a profound influence on Edwards's thought. The nature and extent of that influence has been the subject of recent discussion, and in view of this fact it will be helpful to pay some attention to those points at which Edwards invoked Locke's ideas and explicitly discussed them.

The boundaries of the discussion can be marked off at the outset; Perry Miller in his classic book, *Jonathan Edwards* (1949), was the first scholar to show in some detail Edwards's debt to Locke, but he tended to minimize the points at which Edwards disagreed with him and this gave rise to the belief that Miller had exaggerated the influence. We must bear in mind at this point that Edwards was unique among Puritan thinkers in his philosophical knowledge and ability; no one of his contemporaries was thinking as he was in terms of the laws of Newton or the 'simple ideas' of Locke. Moreover, Locke was bound to appear as something of a foreign body in the theological circles of the time; he was, after all, regarded as a 'mere Deist', and in any case the question was, what was Edwards doing by putting so much stock in such a thinker at the same time he was attacking the much revered Isaac Watts for his erroneous views about human freedom? This anomaly has not been without its effect in the subsequent discussion about the relation of Locke to Edwards. There has been a subcurrent of thinking that Locke should not (could not) have been that important in the development of Edwards's thought, with the result that a reassessment was called for. More recent considerations of the matter have tended in the direction of modifying Miller's view by calling attention to issues

where Edwards dissented from Locke and followed his own bent. As a summary judgement, one can say with confidence that Miller's view is on the whole accurate, but that it is necessary to take seriously the extent to which Edwards read Locke critically and was by no means a mere camp follower.[1]

In order to make the needed comparisons, we shall, of course, have to deal with Edwards's own writings together with those of Locke. Fortunately, we have as well the work of Paul Ramsey and of Wallace Anderson, both of whom have paid special attention to the relationship. Ramsey has concentrated on those parts of Locke's thought which bear essentially on the nature of the will and freedom, and on the considerations of good and virtue which determine moral choice. Anderson's focus is on certain important points concerning the mind, ideas, experience, knowledge and truth, all of which have their own bearing on Edwards's view of human nature and freedom.[2]

Ramsey's work is especially important since he focused especially on the bearing of Locke's philosophy on the development of Edwards's argument in the *Freedom of the Will.* To begin with, Ramsey points out that Locke and Edwards are in agreement that the question whether the *will* is free is a question 'badly posed'. The reason is that the 'will' is not itself an agent, but rather the capacity of an agent. It is the *bird* and *not* the bird's power of flying that has the power. Hence, the question should be whether the *man* is free, and the question whether the *will* is free should be dropped. Edwards, as Ramsey makes clear, agreed with Locke's point, but he tended to forget it in the midst of his polemic against the Arminians who did focus the issue as the freedom of the *will.* This focus was made to order for Edwards and he could not resist shifting the question; as often as he reminded his readers that the question is whether the man is free, he nevertheless continued to direct his criticism against the doctrine that the will is free. The shift enabled him to use the argument, the germ of which is to be found in Locke's analysis, that if the will is to be free, behind every act of will there must be another act of will, and so on without end. This infinite regress, said Edwards, shows the incoherence of the free will doctrine and thus it is destroyed.

Despite this redirection of the argument as a result of the polemical situation in which Edwards was engaged, the fact remains that he agreed with Locke in the need to reformulate the question. Both rejected the prevailing faculty psychology—thought, emotions, will—in favour of the unity expressed by Locke in the term 'mind' and by Edwards in the term 'man'. The point is highlighted when we consider that in Augustine, for example, there is a contradiction in the *will* which is the source of sin while, for Edwards, the opposition between love of God and the qualified love of the natural man is found within the *man* considered as a unity. Edwards, however, went beyond Locke in stressing the unity, partly because his New England opponents held on to the faculty psychology and Edwards feared that they would thus succeed in smuggling freedom, so to speak, back in again.

One of the points at which Edwards disagreed with Locke concerned his account of 'uneasiness' as determining the will. Ramsey has discussed the issue and we shall first turn to what he has to say and then go on to further comment by Anderson who, of course, had the benefit of Ramsey's work in addition to his own study of this and other issues in Edwards's relation to Locke.[3]

As stated in the first edition of the *Essay*, Locke saw 'the greater good [as] that which determines the will', and Edwards expressed agreement with that view. In the second edition, however, Locke altered his position and stressed not the greater good, but 'felt uneasiness' as the motive in willing. Edwards objected to this shift, but, as Ramsey points out, not explicitly because he aimed to *combine* the motivations to voluntary action with the appearance of good to the mind. Edwards claimed to be speaking only of 'the direct and immediate object of the act of volition', which is to say that he brought together what Locke had distinguished. On Locke's view, there is a difference between the greatest apparent good (which, though objectively good, may be remote and on that account unappealing) and the good that makes itself felt in uneasiness or dissatisfaction. The reason for Edwards's conflation of the two is found in one of his original ideas: it is the 'greatest apprehension' of good that determines the will, by which Edwards means that good is apprehended not only by a *judgement*, but by 'having a *clear* and *sensible* idea of any good'.[4] The importance of apprehension for Edwards is made even clearer in the following statement:

> It is not that which appears the greatest good, or the greatest apparent good, that determines the will. It is not the greatest good apprehended, or that which is apprehended to be the greatest good, but the greatest *apprehension* of good. It is not merely by judging that anything is a great good that good is apprehended or appears; there are *other ways* of *apprehending* good.[5]

One of these 'other ways' is to have a clear and sensible idea of any good. Thus, Edwards concludes, 'The degree of apprehension of good, which I suppose to determine the will, is composed of the degree of good apprehended, and the degree of apprehension'.[6] Judgement, though essential, remains a 'dry light' unless it is accompanied by a sensible apprehension; as has been pointed out, this view is original with Edwards and is not to be found in the Puritan tradition he inherited.

Anderson further clarifies the point at issue by offering a more explicit account of what Edwards meant by pleasure and pain, and his consequent divergence from Locke. To begin with, Edwards rejected outright the traditional distinction between the will and the affections, as can be seen both from the *Religious Affections* and in his 'Subjects to be Handled in the Treatise of the Mind'.[7] In the latter somewhat sketchy outline, Edwards set out to discuss 'how far the love of happiness is the same with the faculty of the will; it is not distinct from the mere capacity of enjoying and suffering, and the faculty of will is no other'. In 'The Mind' (No. 67), we find an account of pleasure and pain which is totally at odds with Locke's view and which helps to explain why Edwards had difficulties with Locke's conception of the place of uneasiness:

> Pleasure and pain are not properly ideas . . . Though pleasure and pain may imply perception in their nature, yet it does not follow that they are properly ideas . . . There is an act of mind in it . . . All acts of the mind about its ideas are not themselves mere ideas.

Here Edwards is making place for an *affective* response by the person which goes beyond a merely 'notional' understanding. 'Pleasure and pain', he writes again, 'have their seat in the will, and not in the understanding. The will, choice, etc. is nothing else but the mind's being pleased with an idea . . .'

At this point, we must take note of Edwards's emphasis on tendencies, inclinations and habits of mind; these point to human *capacities* to respond in certain ways which endure and are not exhausted in some finite number of *particular* responses. Edwards, like Charles Peirce later on, fastens upon one of the shortcomings of the British empirical tradition, namely, its particularism and refusal to take seriously the tendencies of the human mind. A tendency is not the same as a particular response, and there seems to be no singular 'impression' or 'sense original' for the enduring habit. Anderson puts the point very well when he says, 'It is clear that Edwards understands pleasure and pain in general,[8] not as being perceived states or sensations in the mind, but as being intentional acts; pleasure and pain are the acts of being pleased or displeased *with* or *in something* that is perceived or contemplated'.

This view of the matter makes it clear why Edwards was critical of Locke's appeal to 'uneasiness' as a motive force. Locke considered uneasiness as a felt state of mind, *antecedent* to the act of will and *distinct* from it; whereas, for Edwards, uneasiness is a disposition or act of the will itself and hence, *ipso facto*, it is a determining factor.[9] The following passage from 'The Mind' makes the difference between Edwards and Locke on this point quite clear:

> That it is not uneasiness in our present circumstances that always determines the will, as Mr. Locke supposes, is evident by this: that there may be an act of the will in choosing and determining to forbear to act or move when some action is proposed to a man, as well as in choosing to act. Thus, if a man be put upon rising from his seat and going to a certain place, his voluntary refusal is an act of the will which does not arise from any uneasiness in his present circumstances.

Another significant point at which Edwards's thought intersects with that of Locke concerns the idea that the will is determined by the 'last dictate of the understanding'. Both thinkers were in agreement about the general proposition, but they differed over the way in which that dictate is determined. This difference is partly terminological, but not entirely so. Much depends on whether the *remote* good is included or excluded from the *present* apprehension of the greater good. Edwards excludes from the present apprehension the remote good, unless it is clear that it plays an efficacious part in the present apprehension itself. Edwards's point becomes clearer if we understand what he means by an object of volition 'appearing agreeable to the mind', and what conditions serve to determine this apprehension. He cites three factors that lead to an object 'appearing agreeable'. First, that in the object—'viewing it as it is in itself'—which makes it beautiful or pleasant, deformed or irksome, to the mind; second, the apparent degree of pleasure or trouble connected with the object and its consequences taken as belonging to the object; third, and most important, whether the apparent pleasure or trouble is 'nearer or farther off'. Since, says Edwards, ''Tis a thing in itself agreeable to the mind, to have a pleasure speedily', the circumstance of *nearness* will be the decisive factor in cases where the agreeableness of two objects viewed in themselves and apart from circumstances is equal; 'the nearer will appear most agreeable, and so will be chosen'. In short, the motive force of a remote good depends upon its being brought within the compass of a present apprehension.

Edwards then applies this analysis to the matter of the 'last dictate of the understanding':

> It appears from these things that in some sense, the will always follows the last dictate of the understanding. But then the understanding must be taken in a large sense, as including the whole faculty of perception or apprehension and not merely what is called reason or judgment.[10]

Edwards goes on to say that if by the last dictate of the understanding is meant what reason declares best for the person's happiness over an entire course of life, it is *not* true that the will always follows this dictate. This is because a dictate of reason 'is quite a different matter from things appearing *now* most agreeable'. For Edwards, the dictate of reason is to be put on the scales as *one* of the determining factors in volition, but it may be outweighed by other factors and so the will may come to be determined in opposition to it. In summarizing this discussion, Edwards does not refer to any dictate of reason or understanding as determining the will but rather to the 'strongest motive'—the position he took at the beginning—'that the will is always determined by the strongest motive, or by that view of the mind which has the greatest degree of previous tendency to excite volition'. It is important to note that, for Edwards, what qualifies a motive as 'strongest' depends on 'the whole faculty of apprehension' and not only judgement; moreover, the self as a living unity must be taken into account, as is evident from his appeal to the strength of a *previous tendency* or habit in the total makeup of the person.

One of the most curious chapters in the story of Edwards's relation to Locke concerns the possibility of *suspending* action and the stress placed by Locke on this power in his revised view of freedom.[11] 'This [power]', said Locke, 'is the hinge on which turns the liberty of intellectual beings . . . the great inlet and exercise of all the liberty men have', that is, 'to hold our wills undetermined.' The issue here is not only one of substance, since Edwards clearly rejected this view on the ground that suspension is but another act of willing. It is rather, as Ramsey puts it:

> The striking and puzzling thing about Edwards's *Inquiry* is, that, with all this before him in Locke, he nevertheless introduces the theory of suspension quite anonymously, as if it were a formulation or possible objection he himself had made up . . . in order to assist and complete his own argument. Why does Edwards not single out Locke for refutation?

Ramsey does not explicitly answer his own question, and indeed there is no way of knowing why Edwards exhibited, in Ramsey's phrase, 'an extraordinary reticence' in the matter. Edwards, instead, went on to attack Daniel Whitby, one of his three antagonists in the *Freedom of the*

Will, and focused on his version of the suspension theory of liberty for refutation. In so doing, Edwards unleashed his most powerful argument—for which he was also dependent on Locke—namely, the claim that to find a will behind every act of willing 'drives the exercise of freedom back *in infinitum*; and that is to drive it out of the world'. To run this sort of freedom 'out of the world' was, of course, Edwards's basic concern, since he was convinced that to allow any 'secondary causes', any power other than that of God in the world, means that God is driven out.

Edwards, bent above all else on overturning the tables of the Arminians, seems not to have been concerned about whether his treatment of the Arminian conception of the will is consistent with his own claim that God always treats the creatures in accordance with their own intrinsic natures. The Arminians continued to insist that Edwards's determinism placed human beings on the same level as stars and stones. Edwards's only reply was to stake everything on the distinction between *moral* and *natural* necessity, so that the former distinguishes moral agency from the actions and reactions between things. In the end, however, despite his claim to be considering whether the *man* is free, Edwards was really asking, as Ramsey rightly says, the question whether the *will* is free.

Edwards could, and indeed did, deal with philosophical and theological questions in their own terms as matters of universal import. He seems not, however, to have been sufficiently aware of the restrictions imposed by polemical discussion where one is inevitably forging a position determined in part by the views one is trying to refute. As Hegel saw so clearly, a dyadic opposition between philosophical positions determines *both* sides of the relationship; this is the reason why so many disputes from the past seem futile in retrospect when a position that was once the object of refutation no longer has any advocates. *Freedom of the Will* and *Original Sin* were both polemical treatises, and the doctrines of Edwards's opponents—Chubb, Whitby and Watts in the former, and Taylor in the latter—left their mark on his response. Edwards's initial intention of considering the freedom of man and not of the 'will' was subverted by the Arminians having posed the question as one of will, and Edwards followed their lead. The curious fact is that Arminius himself spoke of *man* and *self*-determination rather than of freedom of the will, but this emphasis was lost on his followers.[12]

The influence imposed by the polemical context is most evident when we compare both *Freedom of the Will* and *Original Sin* with the *Religious Affections*. In the latter work, Edwards was dealing directly with the religious life, the fruits of the Spirit, the makeup of the individual, the nature of the affections and their validity, all in relation to the Great Awakening. Edwards, of course, had opponents in mind, but the *Religious Affections*, unlike the other two treatises, was not a polemical book; Edwards was free to develop his own position without being confined by the need to argue against the views of particular thinkers. In this respect, *Religious Affections* is the superior work, but it has been neglected by philosophers especially because, unlike *Freedom of the Will*, it is not focused on a standard philosophical issue.

Consideration of Edwards's relation to Locke must include an account of a most important point about which the two were sharply divided, the meaning of 'self-identity'. In 'The Mind' (No. 72), Edwards explicitly questions the view that sameness of consciousness and of memory are sufficient for self-identity. Although Edwards, as in the matter of suspending action, does not mention Locke by name as he had done two sections earlier in connection with uneasiness, his language clearly echoes what Locke says on the topic in Book II, chapter 27 of the *Essay*. 'Identity of person', Edwards writes, 'is what seems never yet to have been explained.' He continues:

> It is a mistake that it consists in sameness or identity of consciousness, if by sameness of consciousness be meant having the same ideas hereafter that I have now, with a notion or apprehension that I had them before, just in the same manner as I now have the same ideas that I had in time past by memory. It is possible without doubt in the nature of things for God to annihilate me, and . . . to create another being that shall have the same ideas in his mind that I have, and with the like apprehension that he had had them before in like manner as a person has by memory; and yet I be in no way concerned in it, having no reason to fear what that being shall suffer, or to hope for what he shall enjoy . . . Will anyone say that he, in such a case, is the same person with me, when I know nothing of his sufferings and am never the better for his joys?[13]

Edwards questions the adequacy of Locke's view because of his own belief that the identity of a person is the result of God's continuous creation at each moment. As is clear from the foregoing, if identity were a matter of sameness of consciousness and memory, God could fulfil these conditions in two numerically distinct individuals, neither of whom would know the other. Hence, Edwards concludes, identity of person must mean something else and have a different basis. The matter is not a purely theoretical one, since something of great importance hangs on Edwards's refusal to accept Locke's position. The question of what constitutes personal identity figures largely in

Edwards's interpretation of the doctrine of original sin and his conception of that identity is at the heart of his explanation of how the sin of Adam can be imputed to all later human beings as their own. The fact is that Edwards offered an entirely original interpretation of the most perplexing feature of the doctrine of original sin: How is one to connect in any intelligible way the disobedience of Adam with all of his descendants?

Edwards was well acquainted with the two dominant answers to this question and he did not accept either of them. On the one hand, there was the position of Augustine which Calvin adopted, and, on the other, there was the doctrine of the Federal theology devised by the founders of American Puritanism. According to Augustine's position, the sin of Adam is transmitted through procreation from parents to offspring after the fashion of an inherited virus so that no one remains untouched by Adam's fall. Proponents of the Federal theology, on the other hand, aimed to improve on this rather crude view by adopting a legal model according to which Adam was conceived as the legally appointed representative for the race. God entered into a *contract* with Adam—the covenant idea drawn from the Old Testament was enormously influential in New England—based on the agreement that as Adam should merit, so his constituents would be treated. Miller has put the essence of this idea very well: 'When he [Adam] fell, his guilt was imputed to his heirs as a liability on the human estate', an arrangement that must have seemed crystal clear to both lawyers and those whose business was the management of goods and property.[14]

We need not deal at this juncture with Edwards's own solution to the problem as he worked it out in his polemic against the English Nonconformist, John Taylor of Norwich, a writer whose work Edwards began to study about 1748. Our concern here is with Edwards's need to set aside Locke's view on personal identity in order to present a new view. To begin with, Edwards had for some time been thinking that there must be some connection between the identity of individuals and the continuity of sin throughout the ages. It was not, however, until 1758 when *Original Sin* was published that he finally determined what the connection is.

Taylor's explosion of the Federal theory of imputation was much to Edwards's liking, since he had never accepted it in any case.[15] Edwards, however, was even more opposed to the grounds on which Taylor rejected the theory, but this was not a proper occasion for Edwards to frame his own view. The idea of a representative whose guilt is imputed to us, wrote Taylor, 'is one of the greatest absurdities in all the system of Corrupt Religion'.[16] He added, in true Arminian fashion, 'neither can any corrupt my nature, or make me wicked, *but I myself*'. This individualistic nominalism, Edwards could not accept. Following his empirical bent, and his awareness of the widespread tendency to evil manifested in human history, Edwards could not see that such a phenomenon could be explained by a discrete series of individual decisions and actions. There must be, he thought, a deeper principle at work; one that would account for the continuity of human wickedness over the centuries.

Edwards's resolution of the problem was in the form of one of his most inspired ideas: Adam, he argued, is connected not with this or that individual here or there, but with *mankind* through the continuously recreative and sustaining power of God who makes each individual identical with him:

> There is no identity or oneness in the case but what depends on the *arbitrary*[17] constitution of the Creator; who by his own sovereign establishment so unites these successive new effects, that he *treats them as one*, by communicating to them like properties, relations and circumstances; and so leads us to regard and treat them as one.[18]

Thus, each person subsequent to Adam is united to him in the same way that the identity of each person from moment to moment is brought about by the divine constitution. The expression 'successive new effects' in the above passage includes *both* the identity within each individual *and* the identity of each individual with Adam. The central point, acutely grasped by Anderson, is that Locke's theory of identity through the same consciousness and memory is inadequate, since 'Edwards certainly did not suppose that God unites us with Adam by giving each of us the same conscious memory of Adam's sinful action as being our own'.[19]

Here everything depends on Edwards's philosophical *realism*, and his insistence on the reality of mankind as a real genus that is not to be construed as a mere collection of individuals. Just as Edwards repeatedly stressed the unity of the self and its manifestation through an entire course of life and not only in disconnected episodes, he emphasized the unity in which all individuals participate as members of the human race. Since God treats mankind as one, it is through our common humanity that we find ourselves burdened with the transgression of Adam.

Anderson's study of the connections between Edwards and Locke, focused especially on Edwards's essay on the Mind which contains many of his philosophical ideas, brings to light a number of other points of divergence between the two. Anderson notes that in 1718 when Edwards was a student at the Collegiate School—the School was renamed Yale in the same year—the writings of both Locke and Newton were included in the curriculum and, according to the records, they were taught in no other institution at the time. Edwards was thus in the unique position of being exposed at once to one of the major architects of the modern scientific revolution and to one of the primary representatives of the European Enlightenment. In addition to the major points where, as we have seen, Edwards was at odds with Locke—the meaning of pleasure and pain, the role of uneasiness in volition, and the nature of personal identity—Anderson cites several other points at which Edwards did not follow Locke.

Edwards held that each person has an innate moral disposition prior to conscious experience and actions, and this view runs counter to Locke's famous *tabula rasa*, or the mind as a blank sheet of paper upon which experience alone can write. Anderson suggests, however, that the difference between them here is 'not immediately apparent', because in other places Edwards expressed agreement with Locke's contention that *sensation* and *reflection* are the only sources of knowledge. Locke's theory, as Anderson rightly says, does *not* preclude innate dispositions or propensities, but he regards them as different from Edwards's idea of an innate propensity to choose sin, and to infer from an effect the existence of a cause.

The difference between them is due in part to a difference in emphasis. For Locke, the agent is seen as the mind, whereas Edwards put the stress on will or understanding. Edwards, moreover, was not entirely satisfied with Locke's 'step by step' approach—what Locke called 'a plain historical account'—because he wanted to retain the direct or immediate element in the act of apprehension. According to Anderson, Edwards held that the mind's performances are not reflective or procedural, but are the operations of habits, dispositions and tendencies in a regular order. Here Edwards seems to have hit upon the same point made much later by the British philosopher F.H. Bradley in his distinction between having something *before* the mind, and having something *in* the mind. The exercise of habit, for Edwards, is governed by a regular order *in* the mind, but it is not necessary for the structure embodied in habit to be *before* the mind in order for the person to follow the habit.

How carefully Edwards considered Locke's thought and set it in relation to his own ideas can be seen in the following examples. Under the heading 'Abstraction', Edwards emphasizes his difference from Locke in claiming that *all* abstractions cannot be extracted from particulars. Colour or sound, he claims, cannot be so abstracted, because 'from simple ideas nothing can be abstracted'. Thus, for Edwards, the case of simple ideas is different from that of complexes such as a man or a horse. The matter is important in view of the central place accorded by Edwards to Locke's notion of simples. Time and again Edwards appealed to the belief that man is unable to create a new simple idea; that only God can do. Hence when Edwards developed his 'sense of the heart' and declared it to be a simple, he was, in effect, claiming that only God could bring about such a sense in the soul of the believer. It is not difficult to see why Edwards was so confident that the presence of the new sense could be used as a sign of an operation of the Spirit and a reliable mark of genuine religion.

An even more telling divergence from Locke is found in what Edwards says about the nature of knowledge. In opposition to Locke, Edwards says, 'Knowledge is not the perception of the agreement or disagreement of ideas, but rather the perception of the union or disunion of ideas, or the perceiving whether two or more ideas belong together'.[20] In this appeal to coherence, Edwards sees himself as having a ground of assurance in knowledge that Locke does not have, namely, our *inability* to act otherwise in the face of a belief. We *cannot*, says Edwards, *believe* that something happens without a cause, since the two ideas necessarily belong to one another. This dictum was, of course, the mainstay of Edwards's attack on the Arminian conception of freedom which he invariably construed as the belief that something happens without a cause.

It has been necessary to consider Edwards's relation to Locke's thought at particular points in order to arrive at a more balanced picture than was possible before so many of Edwards's writings became available in a critical edition in which quotations and citations have been checked and cross references have been verified.[21] The question now arises: Can we make a summary statement about Edwards's relation to Locke's thought as a whole? To begin with, those familiar with Edwards's use of the works of others are aware that he did not as a rule appeal to them for new ideas or even to consult them for their overall views. Instead, he introduced them for his own purposes and took from them just what he needed. As Miller points out, 'He read other thinkers, not for new ideas, but to check their arguments against his own, and to appropriate occasional pages for his own devices'.[22] The best evidence for Miller's point is found in the *Religious Affections*, where Edwards refers to a larger number of other writers than in any of his treatises. There one often finds that he extracts passages from these writers which fit into his argument, even if on the next page that writer is expressing views that Edwards rejects.

Edwards's use of Locke, however, cannot be fitted into this pattern. Locke's thought had a commanding influence upon him and it cannot be understood merely in terms of supportive quotations and piecemeal borrowings. The impact that reading Locke had upon Edwards was something pervasive, colouring his entire outlook. It was something like what Peirce had in mind when he spoke of the 'spread of ideas'. The influence exerted by an idea like evolution, for example, came from its having permeated the entire culture and was not confined to the particular individuals who had read and understood Darwin. So it was with Edwards and Locke, but on a smaller scale.

That Edwards dissented from Locke at particular points does not affect the force of the total experiential orientation of thought which Edwards encountered in Locke's *Essay*. Central was the appeal to experience and the idea of having a 'sense of' beauty, holiness or love. Edwards, moreover, was greatly attracted by Locke's contrast between the spectator who has only a 'notional understanding' of something, and the person who, 'being in some way inclined', is *engaged* by way of attraction or aversion to the object or act in question. Being engaged, for Edwards, meant making an active *response* in contrast to a spectator who is 'neutral' and passive. If Edwards diverged at all from Locke even at this fundamental level, it could only be in Edwards's having established a more intimate connection between sense and understanding than Locke envisaged. For Edwards, the human responses that he calls affections or will, depending on whether an overall act is involved, must be based on an apprehension (understanding) of the nature of the object and that apprehension must be 'sensible' and not merely 'notional'. That difference is the hallmark of the experiential religion that Edwards defended.

Notes

1 This chapter is aimed at drawing attention to those points at which Edwards and Locke were, or appeared to be, at odds. The more basic influence of Locke on Edwards is treated in the next chapter, on 'Religious Affections'.

2 No discussion of the relation between Edwards and Locke can afford to overlook the complications brought about by the uncertainty that surrounds what editions of the *Essay* Edwards used. The matter is important because Locke made significant revisions in the all-important chapter 'Of Power' (Book II, ch. 21) in the second and subsequent editions. Fortunately, Edwards tells us that in writing *Freedom of the Will*, he used a copy of the 7th edition published in London in 1716 and this would have contained Locke's revisions. On the other hand, there is reason to believe that Edwards had access to the first edition of 1690 as a student, because this edition is listed in the catalogue of books donated by Elihu Yale to the Collegiate School (later Yale) in 1713. As Ramsey notes, if Edwards studied the first edition, that might explain why his thoughts on freedom and will correspond so closely to Locke's 'first thoughts' on the subject, and

also why Edwards does not challenge the considerable changes Locke made in subsequent editions. On the other side of the ledger, in Edwards's notes on 'The Mind', a collection begun most probably in 1723 and composed over the next two decades—long before Edwards wrote *Freedom of the Will*—there are objections to Locke's discussion of 'uneasiness' to be found only in the second and subsequent editions of the *Essay*. For present purposes, it will not be profitable to engage in too much detail; the reader should consult the Introduction by Paul Ramsey to *Freedom of the Will*, *The Works of Jonathan Edwards* 1 (New Haven: Yale University Press, 1957), and by Wallace Anderson to *Scientific and Philosophical Writings*, *The Works of Jonathan Edwards* 6 (New Haven and London: Yale University Press, 1980).

3 Ramsey's discussion is limited to matters connected with *Freedom of the Will*, whereas Anderson's comments have a wider base since the essays he was editing contain Edwards's references to and discussions of Locke's writings on a number of philosophical issues and topics.

4 'The Mind' (No. 21b), italics added. The reader should consult the Introduction by Wallace Anderson to *Scientific and Philosophical Writings*, pp. 133–4.

5 'The Mind' (No. 21b), italics added.

6 Ibid.

7 See *Religious Affections*, pp. 11–17, and *Scientific and Philosophical Writings*, pp. 387ff.

8 This term is precisely what Peirce used when he argued for the reality of the 'general' (not the 'universal', which he regarded as a strictly logical term) in the fabric of things, as opposed to the standard claim of the nominalists that only the *singular* 'exists'.

9 The role played by the ideas of habit, tendency and disposition in Edwards's theory of reality has received brilliant treatment in Sang Hyun Lee, *The Philosophical Theology of Jonathan Edwards* (Princeton, NJ, Princeton University Press, 1988). Lee sees very clearly the antinominalist cast of Edwards's thought in his emphasis on the continuing presence of habit and on the unity of the self throughout a 'whole course of life' as opposed to singular, atomic episodes. Lee, moreover, replies to critics who accused Miller of failing to appreciate the emphasis on habit and dynamism in Edwards's thought. Perceptive readers of Perry Miller, *Jonathan Edwards* (New York: William Sloane Associates, 1949) take note of the fact that his chapter on 'Sin' is prefaced by a representative quotation from Peirce in which Peirce calls attention to the error of nominalism in believing that only individuals are 'real', thus denying the existence of a *genus homo*.

10 Edwards, to be sure, always retained some distinction between understanding and will when he wanted to point out the difference between a 'merely notional understanding' had by a person and that person's being 'in some way inclined' either by attraction or aversion to an object or an option. In *Freedom of the Will*, however, he telescoped the two in order to bring the remote good into the mind's present apprehension, for only in that way can such a good determine the will.

11 The references to Locke's *Essay* in what follows are to Book II, ch. 21.

12 The curious fact is that Edwards, wittingly or not, was actually maintaining a theory of *self*-determination, except that, due to the doctrine of election, the individual has no hand in determining the *nature* of the self that is to do with determining. It is noteworthy in this regard that, while the modern anti-determinist view has been largely that of self-determination in the Kantian sense, those like James and Peirce insisted on a more 'libertarian' conception of freedom just because they were wary of the possibility that the determining self could itself be shown to have been determined by purely external factors.

13 'The Mind' (No. 72); *Scientific and Philosophical Writings*, pp. 385–6.

14 Miller, p. 277.

15 It has often been pointed out that, in Edwards's initial appearance before the New England divines in 1731, the sermon he preached, 'God Glorified in Man's Dependence', no mention whatever was made of the Covenant theology. It is clear that, in declaring God to be 'all' and man 'nothing', Edwards was setting aside any notion of an agreement in which God and man would be 'equals' in the transaction.

16 Miller, p. 278.

17 'Arbitrary' must be understood to mean just that something is *willed*, not that it is capricious, random, subject to no pattern, etc.; in Edwards's view, God's willing is always purposive.

18 *Original Sin, The Works of Jonathan Edwards* 3 (New Haven and London: Yale University Press, 1970), p. 403.

19 *Scientific and Philosophical Writings*, p. 118.

20 'The Mind' (No. 71).

21 Earlier editions of Edwards's work, for example, did not distinguish between paraphrase and exact quotation and no attempt was made to locate the originals of such vague references as 'ch. 2, towards the end'.

22 Miller, p. 46.

3

The Great Awakening and 'Religious Affections'

Edwards was not only the most incisive interpreter and appraiser of the Great Awakening, but, with the possible exception of George Whitefield, he was the most influential of the 'Awakeners'. His revival sermons, of which the well-known 'Sinners in the Hands of an Angry God' is typical, have enormous power due to what Miller has called Edwards's 'rhetoric of sensation'.[1] Words, Edwards insisted, must be the vehicle for communicating *ideas* about things. In comments on the proper form of instruction, Edwards says, 'The child must be taught to understand *things* as well as *words*'[2] and to understand things requires *ideas* about them. Edwards had a genius, brought into play by his study of Locke, for presenting ideas in the most vivid way. Edwards might, however, as Miller has suggested, have taken his cue from the Irish philosopher George Berkeley (1685–1753) when he wrote: 'Whatever ideas I consider, I shall endeavour to take them bare and naked into my view'.[3]

Edwards described his own effort in thinking as aiming 'to extricate all questions from the least confusion of the ambiguity of words, so that the ideas shall be left naked'.[4] Once Edwards had ideas before him in this way, he was able to portray them so that they etched themselves on the minds and hearts of his audience. The following extract from a sermon he preached in his early days at Northampton bears eloquent witness to his rhetoric and shows why he was so successful in creating the fervour of revivalism:

> How dismal will it be, when you are under those racking torments, to know assuredly that you never, never shall be delivered from them; to have no hope: when you shall wish that you might but be

> turned into nothing, but shall have no hope of it; when you shall wish that you might be turned into a toad or a serpent, but shall have no hope of it; when you would rejoice, if you might but have any relief, after you have endured these torments millions of ages, but shall have no hope of it; when after you shall have worn out the age of the sun, moon, and stars, in your dolorous groans and lamentations, without any rest day or night, or one minute's ease, yet you shall have no hope of ever being delivered . . . and that your souls, which have been agitated with the wrath of God all this while, yet will still exist to bear more wrath; your bodies, which shall have been burning and roasting all this while in these glowing flames, yet shall not have been consumed, but will remain to roast through an eternity yet, which will not have been at all shortened by what shall have been past.[5]

We see here the rhetoric of sensation at work, which was always aimed at what Edwards called 'making 'em aware and sensible of their own condition'. In setting forth the meaning of God's wrath and judgement on each individual, Edwards does far more than express the ideas in words; he clothes the ideas with images and thus makes them, quite literally, 'sensible' and, in this instance, terrifying. It is no wonder that he was able to launch, almost single-handed, the revival of 1734 and to play so important a role in the Awakening of 1740.

Controversies have a tendency to oversimplify situations, to exclude subtleties of thought and to turn every issue into a two-sided struggle between opposing standpoints, both of which are cast in such obvious terms that everyone can understand them. Revivalism in America during Edwards's time fits this pattern perfectly. For most, including many of the ministers involved, the lines were drawn neatly with the emotional enthusiasm of a Davenport at one end of the spectrum and the cool rationality of a Chauncy at the other. The issue, in short, was which of the two has the priority, the 'heart' or the 'head'. Edwards stoutly rejected this way of putting the problem and reoriented the discussion in such a way that this dichotomy is overcome. The key concept in his entire analysis of the role of experience in religion is that of 'religious affections'. It is, as we shall see, a complex and subtle idea, far too sophisticated to have played any decisive part in the overheated atmosphere surrounding the controversy raised by the Awakening. In any case, although the idea was in the background of Edwards's mind when he wrote the earlier revival tracts, its fullest expression came too late to have figured in the debate. The *Treatise Concerning Religious Affections* did not appear until 1746, two years after Edwards had declared that the Awakening was dead. The work, nevertheless, has proved to be an enduring one and it is by far the most significant document to have emerged from the 'religious commotions' in New England.

One must approach the *Religious Affections* bearing one *caveat* constantly in mind: Edwards's position will never be understood correctly by anyone who comes to it with some form of a heart/head dualism at hand. If that dualism bedevilled the polemics called forth by the revivals, its assumption has been no less disastrous for the efforts of subsequent commentators to come to terms with the work. If someone proposes, as Edwards did, to transcend the dualism in question, no understanding of his ideas is possible for a reader who insists on retaining it.

Previously we took note of Edwards's earlier writings on the revivals, when it was suggested that the ideas contained in them were brought together and expressed in greater detail in the *Religious Affections*. There are, however, a few points from these other writings which will be helpful in understanding the larger work. The *Faithful Narrative* contains the core of experience that Edwards proposes to interpret and assess; it also introduces for the first time the idea of the 'new sense' which is central to the *Religious Affections*. He met people, Edwards says, who claimed that they had heard the Gospel before and even 'allowed' (gave assent to) its truth, but that with the coming of the new sense or the receiving of a spiritual understanding, they could 'see' its truth. This direct apprehending, stated in the language of the empirical philosophy he had learned from Locke, represents the *original* of the sense of the heart. The *conviction* of the truth or excellency of what is apprehended arising from this sense Edwards regarded as distinctive of a spiritual work.

The *Distinguishing Marks* introduces us to the idea of a sign or a criterion for judging experience. This idea was novel. Edwards sought to justify the use of signs by citing the existence of counterfeit piety in the revivals and hence the need to distinguish the true from the false. This work, in addition, appeals to the distinction between *negative* and *positive signs* which plays so large a role in the *Religious Affections*. Since Edwards devoted an entire section to negative signs in the latter work, much remains to be said about them in that connection. At this juncture we may briefly state the main point, since what he understood by these signs remains the same in both works. Negative signs are happenings or certain of their characteristics which are *not* to be taken as conclusive criteria for judging whether the divine Spirit is present or not. For illustrations, Edwards cites the same sort of phenomena that Chauncy had fastened upon when he came to witness the facts about revival experience—unusual effects on the body, excessive imaginings and visions, 'much noise' about religion, and, not least, all manner of misconduct on the part of those who thought themselves converted. Negative signs prepare the way for Edwards's positive signs in the *Religious Affections*, but they were also meant as a blow to those who used these external expressions as the basis for discrediting experiential religion.

The importance Edwards attached to the idea of negative signs can be seen in *Some Thoughts*, where the subject is brought up again, this time in more technical terms. Here Edwards distinguishes between *occasional causes* or accompanying effects, and a *proper* or ultimate *cause*. Occasional causes are negative signs which, although real enough, are an insufficient basis for judging affections; that is to be done only in terms of proper causes. Once again, the distinction made it possible for Edwards to admit the existence of corruption in the revivals—'enthusiasm, superstition and intemperate zeal'—while finding the true basis for judgement not in these effects but in proper causes. Edwards not only retained this distinction through the *Religious Affections*, but there he amassed so many examples of deceptive and ungracious affections—negative signs—that he was led to the conclusion that experience itself is an insufficient criterion for judgement unless it is supplemented by 'clews' from the Word of God.

Some Thoughts provides us with yet another item of importance to the argument of *Religious Affections*, namely, the identification of true piety with holy affections or the fruits of the Spirit. Examining the experiences manifested in the revivals, Edwards discerned a certain 'uniformity' in them which he took to be a parallel to the New Testament record of the experiences of St Paul. Edwards saw the *love* of God dwelling in the heart; the *joy* of believing; the *peace* of God; the *light of knowledge* of God's glory in Christ, and he took them to be sure marks of the divine Spirit. Edwards called the uniformity he discovered a 'lesson of experience'—if experience has to be supplemented by the Word, that Word itself must find its illustrations in experience. For Edwards the two must always go together.

The *Religious Affections* is a brilliant and sustained effort to deal with the basic problem of 'testing the spirits' and, as has not always been recognized, it is a work of great literary power. It is also a difficult book to grasp which is one of the reasons why so many later 'editors', including John Wesley, found it necessary to rewrite parts of it. The idea seems to have been that Edwards undoubtedly had important insights, but that they needed to be expressed in a simpler way. That, of course, was a great error; Edwards was always in command of his thought and his language and he chose his words very carefully. When, for example, he wished to stress the place of the heart in true religious conviction, he found words like 'assent' or 'allow' too weak and lifeless. A man, he says, may 'allow' that something is so and give assent, but unless he is willing to 'profess' that conviction, there is no heart in it. Doctrine and style flow together; if true religion consists in holy affections, then this message itself must be communicated in an affecting way. Edwards illustrated his point by citing an occasion when he heard a minister preaching about the 'lively things of religion' in what he described as 'a dull and lifeless way'.

The vividness of his prose is nowhere more evident than in the magnificent figure he used to compare the true saints with those puffed up by their heightened emotions. The latter are likened to meteors that flare up suddenly in a blaze of light only to fall back to earth, dark and lifeless bodies. The true saints are like the fixed stars, shining with a steady light forever over the infinite spaces. False piety is, however spectacular, evanescent and cannot endure; true piety, the sense of the heart, is an abiding foundation in the soul.

Much has been said thus far about affections as the core of true religion; we must now come to a closer understanding of what Edwards meant when he used the term. To begin with, he distinguished affections from passions; the latter are inclinations that overpower the individual so that 'it is less in its own command'. To be captive to a passion is literally to be a 'patient', and this runs counter to the active response ingredient in an affection. The distinction is of great importance, because most of Edwards's opponents thought he was defending religious passions at the expense of intellect and they did not understand that by an affection he meant the response of the self to an *idea*, an apprehension of the nature of a thing. There is a temptation to use the term 'emotions' as a synonym for affections, but this is apt to be misleading unless emotion is taken to mean a felt response to an object, event or situation which is called forth by an *understanding* of the nature of the object.[6]

In view of these considerations, it is clear that Edwards chose the word 'affections' advisedly, so that he could give it a clear meaning in accordance with the experience on which it is based. The key to understanding the affections is found in the difference between what Edwards called a 'merely notional understanding' of something and 'being in some way inclined' with respect to the object. Notional understanding—knowing *that* an object is hard or round or that a word has a common meaning—is, so to speak, neutral and without preference one way or another. Being 'inclined'—the figure was used by many philosophers with the image in mind of a scale that is not in balance—means that the person chooses to accept or reject the object, situation, event or even doctrine in question. When Edwards uses phrases like 'the actings of inclination and will' he means choice and judgement primarily and overt action secondarily.[7] In every choice the soul likes or dislikes and, says Edwards, when these inclinations are 'vigorous' and 'lively', the liking and disliking correspond to love and hatred. Affections are the *lively* inclinations and choices which reveal the basic direction of the heart. Edwards struggled to make these necessary distinctions in the fact of his concern to protect the integrity of the self as against the idea of separate 'faculties'. The will, for example, does not will; the person is the one who chooses and we call that capacity the will. Edwards repeatedly says that the 'affections are not essentially distinct from the will', but he also says that 'will' is *inclination expressed in action*, as distinct from the 'heart' which is *inclination expressed in the mind*. Some ambiguity remains, but we shall not mistake his meaning if we think of affections as warm and fervid inclinations accompanied by judgement. This central conception will be amplified and at the same time made clearer as we come to consider how the affections figure in Edwards's account of the signs or criteria for judging them.

Love is the paramount affection in Edwards's view and it plays a dual role; on the one side, says Edwards, 'the essence of all true religion lies in holy love', and on the other, 'love is . . . one of the affections . . . and the fountain of all the affections'. Love, then is the *first* fruit of the Spirit which relates the person to God in a decisive way—the 'sealing of the Spirit'—and it is also the source of the other affections —joy, peace, zeal, hope, faith—which make up the religious life. As always, Edwards goes to the Bible in support of his views; in this case his aim is to bring out the meaning of the love of God—'unmixed'—by contrasting it with the rejection of God, symbolized in the Bible as 'hardness of heart', or the 'heart of stone'. What the hard of heart lack, says Edwards, is simply holy love to God, hence if the rejection of God is the opposite of true religion, holy love must be its essence.

We have already taken note of the difficult position in which Edwards found himself; he was committed, on the one hand, to a defence of affections as the core of true piety, but, on the other, he was also convinced that affections had to be tested. Thus he had to argue that the activity of the Spirit shows itself in the affections of the soul and at the same time to set criteria for judging them. In carrying out this project, Edwards took a bold step; he declared that the hand of Satan was to be seen *both* in the revivals themselves *and* in the thought and activity of those who opposed them. Satan, he claimed, realized how few people there were who understood a religion of the heart, and therefore he sowed tares in the form of false affections that deceived many and led them to believe that they were converted. Satan, according to Edwards's interpretation, was also aware of the great opposition that was raised up against the revivals and so he spread the belief that all affections are an evil. Edwards's point is that in both cases true religion must suffer; on one side it is beset by false affections and on the other by the denial that affections are necessary at all. His solution was the claim that affections are essential, but that the existence of false affections forces us to find criteria for testing them.

Before proceeding to describe the twelve signs of gracious affections, Edwards turns once again to the idea of negative signs and reinforces his previous argument, but in slightly different terms. Here his aim is to show 'what are no certain signs that religious affections are truly gracious or that they are not'. The negative signs are, in short, inadequate as criteria for judging affections and Edwards hopes to show that this is the case by noting certain experiences, chiefly excesses and aberrations, from which we are unable to conclude that the Spirit is present or that it is not. The point becomes clear in Edwards's illustrations. It is no sign that 'religious affections are very great, or raised very high' (*Religious Affections*, p. 127); it is no sign that affections 'have great effects on the body' (p. 131); it is no sign that affections 'cause those who have them, to be fluent, fervent and abundant, in talking of the things of religion' (p. 135); it is no sign that affections 'come with texts of Scripture, remarkably brought to the mind' (p. 142); it is no sign that people have 'affections of many kinds' (p. 147). For Edwards, these signs are all external and unreliable as a basis for judging affections.

Edwards adds two more signs to his list and they are of the greatest importance. The first is his rejection, as a negative sign, of the widely held belief that the Spirit follows a certain *order* in its operations; the second is his claim that the judgement of *other people* that affections are gracious or not is not a valid criterion. With respect to the idea of an order of operations, Edwards wants to make one basic point: 'We are often in Scripture expressly directed to try ourselves by the *nature* of the fruits of the Spirit; but nowhere by the Spirit's *method* of producing them' (p. 162). There is indeed a pattern in the way God deals with men, and Scripture gives evidence of God's having first convicted, distressed and terrified man by the contrast between his sin and the majesty of God, and then comforting him with glad tidings. It is not a sign of the genuineness of comforts and joys that they come *after* terror and fear of hell, because being afraid of hell is not the same as having sincere convictions of conscience. Moreover, says Edwards, if there were terrors and convictions actually produced in the soul by the Spirit, that would not prove that comfort *must* follow, for the 'unmortified corruption of the heart may quench the Spirit of God' (p. 157).

Edwards dealt his greatest blow to the belief that the order of operations is a sound criterion in claiming that Satan can *exactly imitate the order* of affections, but not their nature. 'The nature of divine things is harder for the devil to imitate, than their order' (p. 159). If, however, Satan can counterfeit the order, that feature cannot be a reliable and decisive sign. This view, of course, ran counter to a long-standing belief in the Puritan tradition according to which salvation involves a sequential process with distinct steps. In defending his position, Edwards appealed to experience as well as Scripture; he addressed those ministers 'who have had much occasion for dealing with souls' and asked them whether there haven't been 'many who don't prove well', but who, nevertheless, 'have given a fair account of their experiences, and have seemed to be converted according to rule . . .' (p. 160). In summing up his position on this admittedly delicate subject, Edwards made a point of stressing the two sides of negative signs. The presence of an order is 'no certain sign', he says, that the person is converted and, conversely, the absence of an order is not evidence that the person is not converted.[8]

The second major issue raised by Edwards in his extended discussion of negative signs is the attempt to appeal to the 'approval of the godly' as a basis for judgement about a person's spiritual state. Edwards rejects this appeal and in a resounding way. There is, he says, no power given to any person for discerning the heart of another; 'man looketh on the outward appearance, but the Lord looketh on the heart' (1 Sam 16:7). 'It is against the doctrines of Scripture', Edwards says, 'which do plainly teach us that the state of others' souls toward God, cannot be known by us.' Consequently, whatever self-examination takes place on the basis of the positive signs of gracious affections, is to be done by the self for itself; no one can make a final judgement on the state of another person.

Earlier on, mention was made of a possible contradiction between Edwards's rejection of the judgement of others as valid criterion and the 'public charity' that formed the basis for the acceptance of a new church member by the others; the problem became even more acute when Edwards insisted on a public profession of Christ as a condition for being admitted to Communion. What does the 'acceptance' of that profession imply? Does it involve the judgement of others on a person when they 'accept' the profession as a sign of his or her sincerity? Edwards's position on the qualifications for Communion can be made consistent with the doctrine laid down in the *Religious Affections* only if the congregation, in accepting the profession, does not suppose that this is the same as having certain knowledge of the person's state. This is indeed the line that Edwards took in resolving the problem and it gave him an additional argument at the same time. If the heart is known only to God, then the approval of the congregation is not itself a reliable sign for judging religious affections.

Having given a general account of the nature of affections and their central place in religion, together with the negative or unreliable signs, Edwards went on to the largest part of the work, which is a detailed description of the twelve positive and valid signs. There he was able to give a closer analysis of the affections, their relation to ideas and their connection with what he called spiritual understanding.

In approaching the positive signs, it is important to take note of Edwards's use of the generally accepted distinction between the 'common' and the 'saving' work of the Spirit. The *Religious Affections* is concerned only with the latter; the common operations of the Spirit Edwards discussed earlier in the *Distinguishing Marks*. How much he was concerned over the possible misuse of the signs is seen in his prefacing the description of the first sign with a reminder of what he had said previously about not using the signs to judge others: 'It was never God's design to give us any rules, by which we may know, who of our fellow-professors are his, and to make a full and clear separation between sheep and goats' (p. 193). Edwards goes even further; the saints themselves do not have certain knowledge of their state. The signs are, to be sure, available, but corruption and the clouding of the mind make the process of judgement a precarious one. The standards for judgement are themselves secure, but their application to the experience of any individual is not infallible. Here Edwards is stressing the point that no biblical principle is on the same level with its application.

Although Edwards had made many references to signs in the two opening Parts of the work, it is not until Part III, dealing with the positive signs, that he makes fully clear what he meant by signs. A sign is a mark of the presence of the Spirit in the person. Edwards does not say that we *infer* the presence from the sign, but rather that the sign 'points to' the presence, in what we may call the order of knowledge. In themselves, and apart from their evidential force, the signs *are* the presence of the Spirit. The unmixed love of God itself, for example, *is* the indwelling of the Spirit. This point may be confusing since the signs differ in nature; they may be a quality of life, a habit, or a series of deeds extending over time. Edwards, moreover, pays attention to three 'directions' in connection with signs; in some cases the direction is the affection itself, in others the emphasis is on the ground of the affection or what calls it forth, and in still others, Edwards's concern is with the consequences or what issues from an affection. These directions do not receive equal treatment in every sign.

One distinction can be said to cut across all the signs; the difference between the Spirit as 'operating upon' an individual, and as 'dwelling within' an individual. In this way Edwards draws the line between the common and the saving activities of God. The full meaning and force of this distinction is made clearer in Edwards's treatment of the individual signs.

FIRST SIGN

Under this heading Edwards sets forth the basis for the entire analysis. Affections are genuine only when they are 'raised'—Edwards's favourite term—by 'influences' that are *spiritual*, *supernatural* and *divine*. The third of these is actually the coincidence of the other two. By 'spiritual' Edwards meant the special relation of the self *as a whole* to God. Edwards is careful to point out that by 'spiritual' is *not* meant 'what relates to the spirit or soul of man, as the spiritual part in opposition to the body' (p. 198). Edwards is, of course, thinking of what is spiritual in the biblical sense in which it is said to be opposed, not to the body, but to the *natural man*. The point is reinforced when he continues by drawing the line between the activity of the Spirit in relation to the natural man and the redeemed. The natural man is subject to the operation of the Spirit; only in the redeemed does the Spirit dwell within the person in accordance with its own nature. Edwards clothes the distinction with an image of light—a favourite figure in the Augustinian tradition—and contrasts a dark body that has no light except what shines on it from the outside, with a spiritual being whose light comes from within or, as he calls it, a 'lightsome body'.

By 'supernatural' Edwards means what is created by God in the soul and what is beyond the power of the natural man to bring forth. Edwards illustrates his meaning here by citing what is no less than the most important and original idea in the entire treatise: there is in the redeemed a new inward perception, a new simple idea—the sense of the heart—which is a new creation that the natural man does not have. This notion will be developed, sharpened and deepened in the course of the description of the other signs. At this juncture Edwards simply introduces his basic insight:

> So this new spiritual sense is not a new faculty of understanding, but it is a new foundation laid in the nature of the soul, of a new kind of exercise of the same faculty of understanding. So that new holy disposition of heart that attends this new sense, is not a new faculty of will, but a foundation laid in the nature of the soul, for a new kind of exercises of the same faculty of will. (p. 206)

This passage requires careful interpretation; the change brought about by the Spirit is a new foundation in the self as a whole, so that it is not a new understanding or will that comes into being but rather a *new basis* for the exercise of these powers, while the powers themselves retain their integrity. Here Edwards can be seen joining the long tradition of theologians who maintain that grace, though different from nature, is yet continuous with it; the finite can bear the infinite and grace works through created structures. This is not to say that the human faculties remain exactly as they were before; the natural man does not have the same affections as the saints and he cannot will as they do. The main point in Edwards's conception is that the new sense affects the self as a unity that may be expected to manifest itself in all that the person feels, thinks and does. If Edwards at times overemphasizes the discontinuity between the new creation in the soul and anything that the natural man can achieve, it is because of the need he saw to identify affections with what Satan *cannot* counterfeit. We must remember that Edwards needs to use the signs as tests of what is genuine.

SECOND SIGN

Here Edwards's aim is to single out an affection—the pure love of God—which arises entirely from the perception and contemplation of God's glory without any regard for what benefit such love might bring. Edwards insists on the apprehension of God and Christ viewed 'in themselves' which is to say that there are to be no 'conditions' attached; love to God must be 'unmixed'. ''Tis unreasonable', says Edwards, 'to think otherwise, than that the first foundation of a true love to God, is that whereby he is in himself lovely, or worthy to be loved.' Edwards is not unaware of the existence of self-love, but he denies that it can have any determining force in a love to God that is based on an apprehension of the intrinsic loveliness and 'excellency' of God.[9] The love that the individual has for God, says Edwards, cannot be *consequent* upon the belief that God loves him or has forgiven him; love and forgiveness are fruits flowing from the divine goodness and anyone who takes these rewards into account beforehand has a love that is not evoked by a sense of the intrinsic nature of God. As we shall see, Edwards laid great store by his appeal to the intrinsic nature both of the affections and whatever calls them forth; the reason is simply his belief that, whatever Satan has the power to counterfeit, he is unable to simulate an intrinsic nature. Satan cannot simulate holy love because he has none.

THIRD SIGN

Focused on the 'amiableness' of God and the 'loveliness of the moral excellence of divine things', this sign makes an important addition to the preceding one. The importance of the *aesthetic* dimension of experience for Edwards now comes to the fore.[10] This feature of reality and our experience of it was, to be sure, not much emphasized in the Puritan tradition Edwards inherited and its presence in his own outlook went unrecognized until this century, largely because of the prevalence of the stereotypes of Puritanism made popular by American men of letters in the last century. 'Puritanical' was the adjective used to describe a frame of mind opposed to beauty, to art and to any delight to be had through the senses. Edwards, to the contrary, made central to his thought the biblical expression, 'the beauty of holiness'. Holiness he translated into 'moral excellency' or the goodness of God as distinct from his 'natural' attributes such as knowledge and power. The true believer loves the 'loveliness' of this excellency for its own sake. The beauty of this holiness is located in God and certainly not in the eye of the beholder—the usual subjectivist view—but Edwards did maintain that only the purified eye can perceive it.

The value of this sign in testing affections becomes clear when we consider that Edwards was trying to express both the nature of God and the ability of the believer to apprehend it. The 'new sense' of which he speaks is the channel for this apprehension. It is not one of the 'five senses' and it is totally misleading to suggest as many have done that this is a 'sixth' sense. The traditional five senses are all correlated with a bodily organ and it will not even do to suppose that the 'heart' is what correlates with the new sense; the 'heart' is not understood as a bodily organ, but is obviously a metaphor for the centre of the self. The new sense is more than an awareness of God, and it goes beyond belief or assent. It is a sense of, a 'taste' of, the divine *gloria* and its beauty; 'this kind of beauty', says Edwards, 'is the quality that is the immediate object of this spiritual sense'. Whoever *cannot* apprehend it has no indwelling of the Spirit. Edwards proposes that an individual make a trial by asking this question: Is my affection raised by a grasp of the beauty of holiness based on the belief that it is something profitable to me, or is its ground the 'beautiful good in itself'? Only in the latter case is all the calculation of self-love transcended and genuine love to God revealed.

FOURTH SIGN

Edwards's talk of a new sense, of a form of apprehension and perception at the root of affections, is likely to be either confusing or misleading unless we grasp the place that understanding occupies in the entire theory. The fourth sign is of great help because it focuses on what Edwards called a spiritual understanding and shows how it is related to the rise of affections. The problem in following Edwards's thought is in its originality and the futility of trying to understand his position by assuming the idea of faculties with reason and judgement as one department, feeling or emotion as another, and will as a third which is distinct from the other two. Edwards was engaged in an attempt to relate these human powers to each other within the unity of the self and, like all original ideas, his conception suffered at the hands of those who tried to understand him in the very terms he was rejecting.

His first point is that all genuine affections are intimately connected with an *understanding* of the intrinsic nature of what we are responding to in being affected. One of his clearest statements of this point is found in the following: 'Holy affections are not heat without light, but evermore arise from some information of the understanding, some spiritual instruction that the mind receives, some light or actual knowledge' (p. 266). Affections unrelated to understanding are not genuine, 'let them be ever so high' (pp. 266–7). What sort of understanding does Edwards have in mind? The answer he gives starts, in typical fashion, with an indication of what it is *not*. He rejected affections based on 'vain imaginings' or vivid visions devoid of any instruction. For him these were of no account. He was no less scornful of experiences in which people claimed that passages of Scripture came to them suddenly as if God were communicating his special favour to an individual in this extraordinary way. The test is the presence of instruction or understanding; if that is missing, no externals will make up for it.

The question now is: What is spiritual understanding? To begin with, it is not the understanding of the natural man, but rather a new basis for the exercise of that understanding. Spiritual understanding 'must consist in . . . a certain kind of ideas or sensations of the mind . . . the sensations of a new spiritual sense' (p. 269) capable of apprehending the beauty and moral excellency of the things of religion. Unlike a 'merely notional' understanding that has knowledge and grasps the meaning of terms but is 'no way inclined', Edwards's spiritual understanding has a *sensible* element in it which involves both the will and the heart. The contrast is between being an *observer* and being a *participant*. It is not to be thought that the understanding loses its integrity on Edwards's view, since it retains the power of judgement through which the whole self becomes intimately related to what the person understands. Edwards adds a new dimension to the Augustinian conception of the mind that is enlightened by the divine Light when he introduces a new sense or taste as a channel of illumination.

On Edwards's view, spiritual understanding is a new creation; we are not to suppose that the natural man and the redeemed both understand the same things with the difference being that the spiritual man actually believes them. It is rather that the natural understanding alone is incapable of properly grasping divine things and it is for this reason that the natural man fails to acknowledge—does not have the 'sense of'—the excellency and beauty of God, Christ and the Scriptures.

We are now in a position to see why Edwards's position was misunderstood by most of his contemporaries. He was attempting to transcend the head/heart dichotomy generally assumed not only by his opponents but by sympathizers as well. For Edwards, the understanding that is 'spiritual' already contains inclination and judgement or the new sense of the heart within it, so that it will not do to assign judgement to 'reason' as Chauncy did, and set both over against the imagination and the heart. Edwards's aim was to retain understanding as a rational criterion, while expanding it to include the sensible element that is the inclination of the heart. The underlying idea is that, since all affections result from a proper *understanding* of the intrinsic nature of whatever evokes them, those who do not have this understanding can have no genuine affections.

FIFTH SIGN

The emphasis here falls on the conviction that arises, or the sense of the truth of religion that stems, from the apprehension of the excellency of God. Actually, Edwards sees the two-sided character of the sort of conviction that is involved. On the one hand, the doctrines of the Gospel are 'undoubted and indisputable' for those who have received the new sense; on the other, Edwards takes note of the element of trust and even the risk that goes along with the commitment when he says that the saints are not afraid 'to venture their all' (p. 296) on religious truths. Conviction, for Edwards, is not a matter of a 'predominating opinion' coming as the result of speculation or of a probable belief in some doctrine, but rather a direct sense 'that it is so'. The *immediacy* that prevails—the proper meaning of the mystical element in Edwards's thought—is seen in an unusual way. It is not that the Spirit simply produces the conviction in an immediate way, bypassing, so to speak, the understanding, because, for Edwards, conviction cannot arise except through understanding: 'The conviction of the judgment arises from the illumination of the understanding: the passing of a right judgment on things, depends on an having a right apprehension or idea of things' (p. 296).

The so-called and often misunderstood 'idealism' of Edwards is to be found precisely at this point: the response or inclination of the person is totally dependent not on a bare confrontation with an object, but on the *idea* or apprehension the person has of its intrinsic nature. So it is with Scripture; in spiritual understanding, Edwards says, 'then is the mind spiritually convinced of the divinity and truth of the great things of the gospel, when that conviction arises, either directly or remotely, from such a sense or view of their divine excellency and glory as is there exhibited' (p. 297). The novel feature in this view is in Edwards's pointing out the relativity involved. In a passage where Edwards shows his talent for introducing a qualification quite unobtrusively, he tells us that the person with spiritual understanding does not judge 'the doctrines of the Gospel to be from God, *without any argument or deduction at all*, but it is without any long chain of arguments' (p. 298, italics added). What this means is that but one step is required; spiritual understanding directly grasps the divine *gloria* in the Scriptures and the consequent conviction is based on that apprehension. Thus Edwards is able to make out the case that the person's conviction is something internal and intrinsic to the Gospel itself and not dependent on the visions, imaginings and raptures that Edwards saw as inauthentic in the reports of revival experiences.

SIXTH SIGN

Puritan theology had long included a distinction between 'legal' and 'evangelical' *humiliation*; both have to do with being humble before God, but the motivation is not the same in the two cases. Edwards described the affection of humility as evangelical when it stems from *a sense of* the majesty and awesomeness of God, akin to Schleiermacher's *Gefühl* of absolute dependence on God. The humility following on a voluntary denial or renunciation of the self, Edwards called legal humiliation. The great difference between them resides in the character of the heart and will. Legal humiliation, says Edwards, is something exacted from the individual in an acknowledgement of one's inability to keep the law—in St Paul's words, 'I had not known sin, but for the law'. Edwards believes, however, that this sense of humility might occur without the person's acknowledging the true majesty of God. Legal humility does indeed convict the conscience, but, for Edwards, this does not go far enough. There must be in addition a *voluntary* acknowledgement of God's sovereignty and moral excellency which signals a change in inclination of the self as a whole.[11]

It is not difficult to see what use Edwards was able to make of this sign as a test of heart religion. He starts with the duty of self-denial, as regards both worldly inclinations and the tendency to self-aggrandizement, and claims that both may be carried out in a merely legal spirit. The danger is in the great temptation to spiritual pride; the person may make a claim on behalf of his or her accomplishments in humility and, in so doing, show that it is not genuine. Edwards, moreover, saw the peculiar force of this danger in pointing out that a person with a genuine concern to perform Christian duty, as distinct from those who are indifferent, is on that account prone to make comparisons with others to his own credit. He had, of course, observed this sort of behaviour in the revivals and he now had his test ready to hand. Not spiritual attainments or great and overwhelming experiences that serve only to evoke self-righteousness, but an acknowledgement of the majesty of God in a love that flows freely. With the new sense of the God 'that has so loved man' before us, even the greatest human love becomes small. For Edwards, it is not just the doctrine that the divine love surpasses all human love, but the *sense of* the smallness of our love by comparison. Speaking against those who were puffed up by thoughts of their spiritual superiority over others, Edwards says, 'he is no eminent saint; but under the great prevailings of a proud and self-righteous spirit' (p. 329).

SEVENTH SIGN

Edwards gives no indication that the order in which he sets forth the signs has any significance, but it may seem odd that so basic a one—a change of nature—should not make its appearance until the middle of the list. From what has already been said about the new sense and the new creature, it is clear that a change of nature is fundamental. The reason Edwards makes a point of emphasizing this sign is his concern to say something specific about conversion. While it is true that religious literature is filled with autobiographical accounts, often moving and sincere, of a particular time when things turned around in an individual's life and a new orientation to God occurred, Edwards is not at all interested in finding some 'moment' when conversion was supposed to take place.[12] His concern is focused entirely on the change of nature involved in the new orientation—a turn to God and away from the corruptions of the world.

For Edwards, the main consideration is that the Spirit establishes a new nature—'an abiding thing'—which manifests itself over a course of time and has permanence. Past sins do not vanish, but they no longer control because they stand related to a new self. The Spirit, says Edwards, does not seize the person in an instant—he was thinking here of the emotional fireworks occurring in the revivals—but dwells after its own nature in the person to form a continuing foundation. Stress on a transformation that is to make itself known over the entire course of life is Edwards's way of branding as counterfeit sporadic and spectacular 'conversions' that, like the meteor, soon burn out and fall to earth as lifeless matter. As we shall see, this sign links up with the last sign—holy practice—and serves to reinforce Edwards's belief that grace is a 'continued conversion and renovation of nature' (p. 343) in a cosmic progress to be charted ultimately in a 'history of redemption'. In making central what is essentially the historic doctrine of the 'perseverance' of the saints, Edwards was striking a blow against all immediate or intuitive apprehension of being 'saved' by making an appeal to a long course of experience not to be judged in an instant.

EIGHTH AND NINTH SIGNS

These may be taken together since each has to do with the moral dimension of religious faith. Drawing chiefly on the virtues mentioned in the Beatitudes, Edwards describes the Christ-like character in terms of love, meekness and quietness of spirit, and he defines the relations between persons in terms of the heart of flesh. He commends, as the proper attitude of the sincere believer to the world, a quiet trust and gentleness, forgiveness, mercy, and love: 'When persons are fierce and violent and exert their sharp and bitter passions, it shows weakness, instead of strength and fortitude' (p. 351). Much of the discussion of these signs is focused on the dangers of corruption in the virtues. True zeal may be confused with a 'pretended boldness for Christ that arises from no better principle than pride' (p. 352). Confessing a fault openly is a 'vastly greater evidence of holy boldness' in a Christian than fierce confrontations with those who mock religion and reproach believers.

Edwards places great emphasis on the need to take pity on the poor and to take measures to relieve those in distress: 'None are true saints but those whose true character it is, that they are of a disposition to pity and relieve their fellow creatures, that are poor, indigent and afflicted'. Edwards set the 'dovelike spirit of Jesus Christ' (p. 355) over against those who retain a 'contrary spirit' and are guilty of behaviour running counter to the Christlike spirit. Edwards takes the opportunity to apply this sign to all who have a distorted view of what true religion means; he clearly has the revivals in mind: 'Some persons place religion so much in certain transient illuminations and impressions . . . and so little in the spirit and temper persons are of, that they greatly deform religion, and form notions of Christianity quite different from what it is, as delineated in the Scriptures' (p. 356).

He even presses the importance of the tendency of gracious affections to soften the heart in opposition to the fear of damnation so much appealed to in revival preaching: 'An holy love and hope are principles that are vastly more efficacious upon the heart, to make it tender . . . than a slavish fear of hell' (p. 360). Edwards reinforces the point by distinguishing between a 'servile fear' and a 'reverential fear'; the former is focused on the self and it is a calculated response, while the fear that is reverential is concerned only with the thought of incurring God's displeasure itself.

In emphasizing the person's basic attitude to the world and his or her behaviour in relation to other people, these two signs point beyond themselves to the last sign, the sign of holy practice. There, as we shall see, the Puritan consciousness is made to come out of the inner recesses of the soul and express itself in a public domain where all can see. With this development the fruits of the Spirit become more visible and tangible, and what Puritan writers called one's 'carriage' in the world becomes a major test of purity of heart.

TENTH SIGN

Gracious affections, says Edwards, differ from false in having 'beautiful symmetry and proportion'. We have already taken note of the paramount importance Edwards attached to the *aesthetic* dimension of religious experience; this sign furnishes further evidence of that importance. The focus here is, however, less on what Edwards means when he speaks of having 'a sense of' God's majesty or of the excellency of the Scripture, than on the beauty manifested in 'God's workmanship'. While the saints are never perfect in the symmetry that pervades their lives, they are free of that 'monstrous disproportion' in affections 'that is very commonly to be observed in . . . the counterfeit graces of hypocrites' (p. 365). As a standard for judgement Edwards cites the 'whole image of Christ' that is upon the new man; there is every grace in [him], 'which is in Christ'. The image of Christ in the redeemed corresponds 'feature for feature' and 'member for member' with that symmetry and beauty to be found in the original. Edwards is looking for a balance and harmony in a total life pattern which is to distinguish the redeemed from the hypocrites in whom there is 'no manner of uniformity in their affections'.

Edwards places great emphasis on what we may call the 'double mourning' for sin present in the saints. Unlike the hypocrites, says Edwards, the saints 'have not only sorrow to prepare 'em for their first comfort, but *after* they are comforted, and their joy established' (p. 366, italics added). The hypocrites, presumably, have only a single mourning and it ceases as soon as, in Edwards's figure, the person has been delivered from captivity and settled in the land of Canaan. The true saints, on the contrary, continue to loathe their sins *after* their deliverance as the children of Israel were commanded to 'feed upon the paschal lamb, with bitter herbs'. Building on this central idea, Edwards goes on to describe a number of 'disproportions' and 'partialities' in people's affections in order to make it possible to judge whether the proper symmetry is present.

Two examples suffice to make his point. First, there is the love of God in relation to the love of one's neighbour. Some profess great love of God and Christ, but show little charity to their neighbours; others are very generous to other men, but show no love to God. Second, there is love to men, and Edwards sees a considerable amount of partiality and discrimination in these relationships. In one of his most telling examples, Edwards takes note of the difference in the attention paid to the outer man as distinct from the soul. Some, he says, will give liberally of their goods to help the poor, but care little for their spiritual welfare. Others do just the opposite; they profess great love to men's souls which 'costs 'em nothing', but 'in order to show mercy to men's bodies, they must part with money out of their pockets' (p. 369).

Edwards took the description of this sign as an occasion for making a most significant statement about the relation between morality and religion, and in terms that make clear his concern about antinomianism: 'If persons pretend that they come to high attainments in religion, but have never yet arrived to the lesser attainments, 'tis a sign of a vain pretense' (p. 370). Here Edwards is castigating those who claim to be beyond morality and living a divine life, except that they have not 'come to be so much as moral persons'. Edwards expresses this judgement in a memorable figure:

> He that is in a journey, and imagines he has got far beyond such a place in his road, and never yet came to it, must be mistaken; and he is not yet arrived to the top of the hill, that never yet got halfway thither.[13]

Edwards follows this declaration with an ironic touch that is typical of his rhetorical power—'But this by the way'. The reader is led to see at once that this is the essence of his condemnation of a false piety that supposes morality to be beneath itself and that, by comparison, the other features of this sign are 'by the way'.

Edwards cannot let the matter of proportion in the religious life go. Mindful of the spectacular and sporadic experiences recorded in the revivals, he attacks those who are 'religious only by fits and starts'. In another memorable figure, this time drawn from nature, he compares the transiency of false affections with the constancy of the saints:

> They are like the waters in the time of a shower of rain, which during the shower, and a little after, run like a brook, and flow abundantly; but they are presently quite dry, and when another shower comes, then they will flow again. Whereas a true saint is like a stream from a living spring; which though it may be greatly increased by a shower of rain, and diminished in time of drought; yet constantly runs.

The contrast between the transient and the enduring here is exactly parallel to the figure in which Edwards compares the hypocrites to meteors that blaze up *suddenly* only to lose their light in a dwindling trail of sparks, and the true saints to the fixed stars whose light is *steady* and *unfailing*.

We must not, however, be misled by the seeming rigidity of these contrasts. Edwards was secure enough in his own position not to have to resort to the simple exaggerations of bad rhetoric. He does not claim that true Christians are always alike and he admits that 'the best have reason to be greatly ashamed of their own unsteadiness' (p. 371). His claim is that there is a 'much greater' disproportion in false affections than in true, which means that even true affections are not without flaw.

ELEVENTH SIGN

Here Edwards harks back again to his knowledge of what happened in the revivals; false affections remain satisfied with themselves and take pride in previous attainments, whereas true piety is accompanied by an increase in spiritual appetite: 'The more a true saint loves God the more he desires to love him, and the more uneasy he is at his want of love to him' (p. 377).

Edwards repeatedly emphasized the dynamic and developing character of the religious life; the more grace abounds, the more true believers become aware of their imperfection. In this sign Edwards connected this awareness with the 'new sense' of the heart, as we see in the following: 'The more persons have of holy affections, the more they have of that spiritual taste which I have spoken of elsewhere; whereby they perceive the excellency, and relish the divine sweetness of holiness' (p. 378). By contrast, those who believe that they have finally been 'converted', says Edwards, simply rest on their laurels, so to speak, and their earnestness in seeking dies out. He took this to be a sure sign; false affections are in those who 'live upon their first work, or some high experiences that are past . . . there is an end to their crying, and striving after God and grace' (p. 380). The trial, however, continues and in the test of endurance those who have the appetite for holiness for its own sake come to stand out as against those whose aim is, as Edwards puts it shortly, 'only for by-ends' or self-gratification.

It is in this and in the preceding sign where the emphasis falls on enduring patterns of life manifest only over a long period of time, that we see Edwards leading up to the final sign—holy practice encompassing the whole of a person's life.

TWELFTH SIGN

It is not without significance that in Edwards's text the discussion of all the previous signs occupies less than two hundred pages, while the account of the twelfth sign extends over some eighty pages. The reasons for so lengthy an exposition and defence of the claim that holy practice is the chief sign of gracious affections become clear when we consider the difficult questions involved. Edwards, as we shall see, had to deal with the perseverance of the saints and the problem of backsliding,[14] the nature of practice and its relation to the other affections, the connection between faith and works, and the compatibility between holy practice and justification by faith. In seeking to accomplish his task, Edwards made the most of his belief that reason and Scripture must go hand in hand and we find him appealing now to one and then to the other in developing what he believed to be the true biblical view of the place of practice in the Christian life.

He begins by taking note of three focal points that structure the entire discussion. The first is that the person's behaviour in the world must always be conformed to and directed by Christian rules; the second is that holy practice is a 'business' which a person 'is chiefly engaged in'; the third is that the person persists in this business to the end of life, or, as Edwards says, it is not the business of a month, or a year, or of seven years, 'but the business of his life'.

The steadfastness of true religion is made manifest in the midst of those trials in the world, those temptations that make it difficult for the person to continue in the performance of duty. These trials, says Edwards, are part of God's design to make clear both to the individual conscience and to the world what strength of conviction a person has. Here Edwards, and without preamble, raises the much discussed problem of backsliding: 'True saints may be guilty of some kinds and degrees of backsliding . . . and may fall into sin, yea great sins: but they can never fall away so, as to grow weary of religion, and the service of God' (p. 390).[15] The new creature in Christ, although still subject to temptations, is sanctified in spirit, soul and body; this new nature, according to Edwards, is permanent.

Critics of Edwards's view claimed that he could admit some degree of backsliding in the case of a true saint, but that he would have to know on other grounds that the person was a true saint. Edwards's response was that a falling away at the root—a habitual dislike and neglect of religion—is the sign that the person was never a true saint in the first place: 'They that fall away and cease visibly to . . . walk in the newness of life, 'tis a sign they never were risen with Christ' (p. 391). Edwards may well have availed himself of the idea of negative signs which he used so effectively in the first part of the *Religious Affections*—backsliding and giving way to temptation would of themselves be no sufficient evidence of false affections. Only a total 'decay and fall off from the Lord' would be the decisive sign. But, for Edwards, such a turning away from God could never be a possibility for one who had really been made a new creature. The one who has really been given grace has no power to resist it.

Those who have received spiritual understanding and the new sense from which to apprehend the excellency in divine things will know that they are 'worthy to be chosen and adhered to'. In Edwards's view, there is a close connection between a conviction of the truth and reality of God's commands and the power to carry them out in practice. Those who were never convinced of this truth 'will never be at the labor and trouble of such . . . persevering practice of religion' (p. 395). Those who are 'thoroughly convinced of the certain truth of those things, must needs be governed by them in their practice'.

The point to be noticed here is that the new nature in the person which stems from grace is no longer being understood as a merely internal transformation. Edwards is well aware, to be sure, that the direction of the heart is not something to be seen, but the holy practice that follows from the new sense of the divine excellency *can be seen* through action in the world. Piety, in short, is coming out of the closet of the mind and showing itself in its fruits of practice where all can see.

Edwards repeatedly refers to a 'practical tendency' and of the power of grace to issue in deeds over a course of life: 'True grace is not an unactive thing; there is nothing in heaven or earth of a more active nature; for 'tis life itself'.

Edwards goes on to claim that, rightly understood, Christian practice 'is the chief of all the signs of grace'. It is the *principal sign* by which sincerity is to be judged. Edwards supports his claim with a battery of biblical citations and declares that 'Christ directs that this light should not only shine within, but that it should shine out before men, that they may see it' (p. 408). Good *works*, he says, are superior to good *words*. It is, moreover, not only a matter of Scripture, because 'reason teaches the same thing'. 'Reason shows that men's deeds are better and more faithful interpreters of their minds, than their words' (p. 410). And in a remarkable parallel, Edwards declares that 'Reason says the same that Christ said, in John 14:21: "He that hath my commandments, and keepeth them, he it is that loveth me" '. That a person strives to imitate Christ and to deny himself for Christ's honour, Edwards continues, is better evidence, in reason's view, of love to Christ than the person's *saying* he has love to Christ and telling of merely inward experiences.

In stressing the saying/doing contrast, however, Edwards is concerned that he be rightly understood. That Christian practice provides the best evidence of sincerity does not mean that 'a profession of Christianity' is excluded. On the contrary, he says, such a profession is presupposed from the outset. Rules of conduct are laid down 'not for the trial of heathens, or those that made no pretense to Christianity', but as guides for the behaviour of professing Christians. Edwards interprets Christ's rule, 'By their fruits ye shall know them', to refer to the fruits of Christian faith. In accordance with his typical thoroughness, however, Edwards does not leave the matter there, but launches into an extended discussion of what it means to make a profession of Christianity. As we shall see, he is leading up to the problem of the proper relation between faith and works.

Two things, Edwards says, are requisite for a proper profession; the first is profession of what is essential to Christianity with nothing left out; the second is that the profession must be made 'understandingly' as the result of instruction in the principles of religion. By essential Christianity Edwards means the belief that Jesus is the Messiah, that Jesus 'satisfied for our sins, and other essential doctrines of the gospel'. The latter include repentance, conviction of sinfulness and a wholehearted acceptance of Christ as saviour. Genuine profession must also include an understanding of the 'proper import of what is expressed in [the] profession' for, as Edwards says, 'sounds are no significations or declarations of anything, any further than men understand the meaning of their own sounds' (p. 416). Sincere profession, then, always involves awareness and experience; people profess 'that they are conscious to, or do experience such things in their heart'.

As regards people relating their experiences to others, Edwards takes the opportunity to reinforce the point he had made not only in the first part of *Religious Affections*, but in other writings as well—a rejection of the idea that the Spirit works in accordance with a fixed order of steps. ''Tis not necessary that they should give an account of the particular steps and method, by which the Holy Spirit, sensible to them, wrought and brought about those great essential things of Christianity in their hearts' (p. 416). The important thing, says Edwards, is a profession of the fruits, but 'no account of the manner of working', because 'there is no footstep in the Scripture'. Here, as before, Edwards was attacking as unbiblical the belief widespread among Puritans that the Spirit works in the soul in accordance with a certain order and that the presence of that order is reliable evidence of the presence of the Spirit.

In order to avoid any misunderstanding about the nature of good works, especially in relation to grace, Edwards offers an analysis of human action. The keeping of Christ's commandments has not to do with what is external, 'the motion and action of the body . . . having no respect to any aim or intention of the agent, or any act of his understanding or will' (p. 422). From that point of view, men's action would be the same as the regular motions of a clock, if indeed it could be called human action at all. When Scripture speaks of obedience and fruit, it is the obedience and fruit of the man, and 'therefore not only of the acts of the body, but the obedience of the soul, consisting in the acts and practice of the soul'. Edwards's point here is that we must not confuse *roots* and *fruits*; holy practice is the fruit which is a sign of the root that is the holy principle in the heart.

In an effort to make himself clearer, Edwards speaks of two kinds of exercises of grace. One is the exercise of grace 'that remains within the soul . . . without any immediate relation to anything to be done outwardly'. The other is the kind of acts of grace 'that are more strictly called practical or effective exercises; because they immediately respect something to be done' (p. 423). The first kind of grace Edwards associates with contemplation or exercises of the heart that do not terminate in anything beyond the mind, even if they ultimately tend to affect practice remotely. The second exercise of grace has to do with the commanding acts of the will; the exertion of grace producing its effect in outward action. The acts themselves, the giving of a cup of water to the thirsty, the enduring of persecution for love of Christ, are essential but they cannot be taken apart from the aim and intention of the soul. Edwards is quite emphatic on this point, as we see in the following:

> For not only should we not look on the motions of a statue, doing justice or distributing alms by clockwork, as any acts of obedience to Christ in that statue; but neither would anybody call the voluntary actions of a man, externally and materially agreeable to a command of Christ, by the name of obedience to Christ, if he had never heard of Christ, or any of his commands, or had no thought of his commands in what he did. (p. 423)

On Edwards's view, when holy practice is meant to be the evidence of the person's true Christianity to others, it is that in the practice which is visible to them—the act itself. When, however, it is a matter of evidence of sincerity to an individual's own conscience, it is not just the motion of the body that counts, but the 'motion and exercise of the soul' of which the act is an expression. As Edwards says, in the evidence of sincerity, 'what is inward is of greatest importance', but what is outward is also included since it is connected with the practical force of grace in the will. In all this Edwards aims to preserve the unity of the agent and the unity of inner and outer; holy practice is the outer expression of the grace that works in the inner man.

Practice has yet another dimension for Edwards; it is 'the most proper evidence of *trusting* in Christ for salvation' (p. 446) Although Edwards presents this idea in a paragraph that is quite dense, his point is very much the same as that of William James when he cited willingness to venture or take on the risk in acting as a reliable indication of a person's trust or dependence on some power or possibility. 'The proper signification of the word "trust" ', Edwards writes, 'according to the more ordinary use of it, both in common speech, and in the Holy Scriptures,[16] is the emboldening and encouragement of a person's mind, to run some venture in practice, or in something that he does, on the credit of another's sufficiency and faithfulness.' The evidence that a person is trusting in Christ in the biblical sense, is the willingness to lose life in order to find it, to 'part with all' and 'venture all' in a dependence on Christ's truth. We see here a further indication of Edwards's concern for a practical and overt manifestation of a person's will and heart. Edwards saw that *saying* that one trusts, even with the most sincere of intentions, may be deceptive and that one needs the test of actual *doing*, not merely as evidence to others, but as an indication to one's own conscience of the presence of actual trust.

Edwards rarely set forth any of his views without a consideration of objections; in some cases, he is responding to contrary opinions expressed by others, but more often than not he is raising possible objections of his own devising in order to make his position clear. In this instance, he is concerned to deal with that opinion, 'so much received among good people', that inward, spiritual experiences are the main evidence of grace instead of holy practice. Edwards's aim is to show not only that the two are not incompatible, but that it is a mistake to regard them as entirely distinct. His main point is an appeal to the unity of the person and his idea of experience as including both mind and will:

> The exercises of grace that Christians find or are conscious to, within themselves, are what they experience within themselves; and herein therefore lies Christian experience: and this Christian experience, consists as much in those operative exercises of grace in the will, that are immediately concerned in the management of the behavior of the body, as in other exercises. These inward exercises, are not the less part of Christian experience, because they have outward behavior connected with them. (p. 450)

In a passage typical of his analytical skill, Edwards goes on to attack any separation between experience and practice: 'all Christian experience is not properly called practice; but all Christian practice is properly experience'. The distinction that some make between the two, he claims, is both unreasonable and unscriptural. Once again, we find Edwards trying to protect his conception of experimental religion[17] from distortion. He was fully aware of the emphasis he had placed on experience and having a *sense* of the things of religion, but he was also concerned that this not be understood as merely 'inward' and divorced from behaviour in the world. Consequently, he insisted on including practice within the compass of experience and thereby retained the moral dimension. The danger, he saw, was in the claim of persons to have what he called 'high experiences', and 'heightened affections' as if these were sufficient, while exempting themselves from the need to express this experience in holy practice.

Edwards's final concern in his presentation and defence of the twelfth sign is to show that his cardinal emphasis on good works is not inconsistent with the doctrine of justification by faith alone. His argument begins with a dramatic note. If, he says, the doctrine of free grace and justification by faith alone are inconsistent with holy practice as a sign of grace, 'then they are equally inconsistent with the importance of anything whatsoever in us as a sign of grace' (p. 456). His point is that all the signs are inconsistent with justification by faith alone, if they are taken as *means of justification* and not, as they should be, as signs of grace: 'To make light of works because we ben't [are not] justified by works, is the same thing in effect, as to make light of all religion, all grace and holiness'. When the Scripture says that we are not *justified* by works, it means by 'works' *our own* righteousness, religion or holiness. What Edwards means by holy practice is works that stem from, and are the sign of, the grace that works within those who are justified by their faith. Gracious affections, including holy practice, are the marks of the Spirit, but no one of them is a means of justification. On the contrary, these affections have their root in the new creature who is justified by faith alone.

Notes

1 'Sinners' is probably the best known of any writing of Edwards and indeed there are those for whom it is his only writing. The importance of this sermon has been exaggerated beyond measure by enthusiastic anthologists, and this is unfortunate because it is by no means typical of Edwards's sermons *as a whole*, even if it is a good example of revival rhetoric.

2 Sereno Edwards Dwight, *Life of President Edwards* (1830), pp. 475–6.

3 *Religious Affections*, Introduction, sec. 21.

4 *The Works of Jonathan Edwards* 4 (New Haven and London: Yale University Press, 1972), p. 278.

5 Ibid.

6 The opposition in common sense between an 'emotion' and 'reason' or 'thought' is based on the assumption that an emotion is a mere feeling that is *not* essentially related to whatever it is that evokes it. For this reason Edwards rarely uses the term; his affections are responses of the self as a whole to an *understanding* of what the person is responding to. Thus 'the fear of the Lord' is not for him a feeling occurring at random, but the affection that arises when one *understands* the glory, majesty and sovereignty of the 'Lord'.

7 See the Introduction by Paul Ramsey to Edwards's *Freedom of the Will*, *The Works of Jonathan Edwards* 1 (New Haven: Yale University Press, 1957), pp. 16ff. where the element of choice or judgement is said to take precedence over exertion, thus explaining why Edwards identified 'volition' and 'preference'.

8 Underlying the entire discussion about order in experience is another issue—the question whether it is possible for a person to 'prepare' the heart for the reception of grace. The matter is quite complex and we cannot attempt to deal with it here; the reader should consult the excellent treatment of the subject in Norman Pettit, *The Heart Prepared* (2nd edn; Middletown, CT: Wesleyan University Press, 1989).

9 For the meaning of 'excellency'—one of Edwards's key concepts—see below, pp. 107, 108, 130–1.

10 We shall return to this topic in more detail in connection with the Tenth Sign which has to do with symmetry and proportion.

11 'Voluntary' needs to be explained at this point. According to Edwards's position in the *Freedom of the Will*, a 'voluntary' acknowledgement of the sort required is possible only for those who have already received the new sense. In short, when the redeemed self is in place, the acknowledgement follows 'voluntarily'.

12 The NT Greek word *epistrephō* and its Latin equivalent *converto* have the same connotation of a 'turning about' or facing in a new direction. Plato uses the term in describing the turn to the light of reality in the myth of the cave.

13 This is a charming, and all the more so because almost certainly inadvertent, illustration of one of Zeno's famous paradoxes generally known as 'half the distance'. In order to travel a mile, one must go as far as a half-mile, and in order to reach a half-mile one must have gone a quarter of a mile, etc.

14 Whether and to what degree true saints were capable of regressing or failing to persevere was a much debated topic. John Wesley, for example, was opposed to Edwards on this point, as he made clear in his 'edited' version of *Religious Affections* that appeared in 1801 in London. See *Religious Affections*, *The Works of Jonathan Edwards* 2 (New Haven: Yale University Press, 1959), pp. 79–80.

15 For biblical support, Edwards cites Gal 6:9; Rom 2:7; Heb 10:36; Is 43:22; Mal 1:13, and adds long passages from Stoddard's *Sincerity and Hypocrisy* (1719) and Thomas Shepard's *Parable* (1660), both of which were well known at the time.

16 It is interesting to note that Edwards does not identify 'ordinary use' with 'common speech', but thinks of it as indicating a *consistent* use in both common speech and in Scripture.

17 Edwards used the expressions 'experimental religion', 'experiential religion', and 'heart religion' as synonyms. He did not use 'religious experience'—the expression made so familiar by William James in *The Varieties of Religious Experience* (1902).

4

Freedom of the will

Freedom of the Will may be seen as a sustained effort by Edwards to become engaged on two fronts at once. On the one hand, he sought to deal with the enduring problem of human freedom in both theological and philosophical terms, and to develop a position having biblical support and the evidence of reason, or, as he sometimes put it, 'common sense'. On the other hand, Edwards had a decidedly polemical intent which was to destroy the position of the Arminians by showing the inconsistencies and difficulties inherent in 'the Arminian notion of liberty of will, consisting in the will's self-determining power'.[1] For this purpose, Edwards took issue with three thinkers—Thomas Chubb, Daniel Whitby and Isaac Watts—who, though differing considerably in their basic standpoints, were regarded by Edwards as united in holding an Arminian view of human freedom and, as a result, in opposing other doctrines upheld by Calvinists.[2]

Since the term 'Arminianism' was used by Edwards and many others as a blanket expression meant to cover a number of doctrines set forth in opposition to the Calvinist tradition, a brief indication of what is to be meant by the term is essential for understanding Edwards's polemic. Arminianism was named after Jacobus Arminius (1560–1609), a Dutch theologian and founder of what was known as the Remonstrant school within the Dutch Reformed Church. His orientation was definitely anti-Calvinist, as can be seen in the following theses that defined his position:

> First, the sovereignty of God is to be understood in a way that is compatible with man's freedom; Second, Christ died for all sinners and not just for the elect, with the consequence that all sincere

believers can have some assurance of salvation; Third, a regenerated person is free to perform and will the *right*.

These theses, to be sure, stood in need of more precise formulation, which was forthcoming in the course of the debate that actually turned on the meaning of freedom itself. And, as we shall see, the polemical situation inevitably led to the posing of questions along fixed and uncompromising lines so that each side in the controversy came to express itself in extremes that do not finally do justice to the fundamental intentions of the opposing positions. Ramsey, it should be noted, has taken account of this factor in claiming that it is a mistake to say that Edwards chose to engage only extreme Arminianism in order to gain a greater victory.[3]

It is fair to say that Edwards set forth his own position in its main features prior to engaging the adversaries he singled out for attack, but it is also true that a number of important details in Edwards's position come to light only in the course of the controversy itself, so that the polemical context makes its own contribution. As we shall see, this contribution is not unimportant, since, among other things, the polemical concern led Edwards to make a fundamental shift in the basic issue; at the outset, it was the freedom of the *man* or the self that was said to be at stake, but in view of the Arminian emphasis on the freedom of the *will*, Edwards was pleased to turn the discussion in that direction instead.

The *Freedom of the Will*[4] is divided into four parts. In the first, Edwards deals with terminology and such topics as the nature and determination of the will, the meaning of necessity, impossibility and contingency, the distinction between natural and moral necessity, and the notions of liberty and moral agency; in the second, he considers whether there is or could ever be any freedom of the sort claimed by the Arminians; in the third, he discusses whether such Arminian liberty is necessary for moral agency, praise and blame; in the fourth part, Edwards deals further with the arguments of his opponents and analyses the divine volition in relation to the world and to man. In a conclusion, Edwards attempts to anticipate the sort of reception the work will have at the hands of anti-Calvinists.

Such an effort is typical of Edwards's approach and not restricted to this occasion. It is as if he were determined to have the last judgement on his work by not sending it out to the world without making his own assessment of what opponents would say and why he thought their objections would be mistaken. Although this conclusion is quite brief—it occupies less than ten pages in comparison with the 430 pages devoted to the main argument—it is most instructive because it signals, in concise form and far more clearly than the body of the work itself, exactly where, in Edwards's view, the battle lines were drawn. The *Freedom of the Will* is an intricate and subtle work and we cannot hope to review it in detail; consequently, a reader will profit greatly from Edwards's summary of what he believed he had accomplished.

Edwards's first concern is to submit what he has written to the judgement of others, but only insofar as his argument is 'liable to any tolerable answer' made on the basis of 'calm, intelligible and strict reasoning'. There is, to be sure, an air of superiority in this seemingly humble approach—Edwards always assumed that he would not be bested in the way of argument—but there is a corrective in the fact that, in comparison with his contemporaries, Edwards had by far the more acute mind. However, having made this appeal to the judgement of others, Edwards tells us that he is 'sensible' that his position is liable to 'one sort of answer'. This answer turns out to be the 'usual exclamations' of those who supposedly rely on rhetoric rather than on logical argument.

Edwards then goes on to rehearse what he takes to be the rhetorical and inflammatory responses by his opponents to a number of his basic doctrines. Thus, he says, there will be expressions of concern for the 'fate' of the heathen in connection with the doctrine that Christ died chiefly, if not only, for the elect.[5] There will be invocations of 'Hobbes' necessity' and the spectre of making men into machines. There will be the use of terrible epithets—'fatal', 'inevitable', 'irresistible' in response to 'irresistible grace', and use of the words 'horrid' and 'blasphemous' with respect to God's being responsible for the damnation of the hypocrites. In addition, says Edwards, opponents of his views will express themselves in ways aimed at inflaming the imagination of those who are either unable or unwilling to examine the matter in a rational way. And this is not all; the enemy will also lay stress on what is irrelevant or diversionary in order to evade the inevitable arguments that demonstrate Edwards's position.

Having dealt with 'procedural' matters, Edwards goes on to the specific doctrines at issue. He states at once his fundamental contention: 'the decision of most of the points in controversy between Calvinists and Arminians, depends on the determination of this grand article concerning *the freedom of the will requisite to moral agency*' (p. 431, Edwards's italics). According to Edwards, establishing the Calvinist position on this point does away with all Arminian doctrine at one stroke since their whole position depends on the supposition of such freedom. Edwards, however, does not leave the matter there, but proceeds to the particulars of the case and in the sequel we see how acute he was in anticipating what the objections would be.

His initial concern is to deal with the presence in God's government over mankind of counsels, warnings, calls, expostulations, promises, rewards and threats, all of which might seem to imply that man has some 'freedom' in responding to these overtures. Edwards's reply is that none of these is inconsistent with 'a determining disposal of all events . . . either by positive efficiency, or permission'. Universal providence, he says, implies 'some kind of necessity of all events', but in the case of moral agency, it is 'moral necessity' that is involved and this, Edwards claims, is not inconsistent with willing of that sort. The point constantly emphasized is that the 'futurity of all future events is established by previous necessity, either natural or moral' (p. 432). What this means for Edwards is that God's immediate conduct, whether in acting or forbearing, is the 'original' in the series of all subsequent events. Despite the great length and the intricacies of Edwards's argument, his position rests, like a huge tower, on one foundation: God alone is *the* cause of all and to allow 'secondary causes' is tantamount to denying the reality of God altogether.

Edwards's next target is the unwillingness of the Arminians to acknowledge the total corruption of human nature. Here he claims to have shown that the main objection to the Calvinist doctrine that man is unable, without grace, to love God 'savingly', is that it is inconsistent with the freedom of the human will and requires man to do what he cannot do. Edwards was quite adept at placing himself inside, so to speak, an objection, even if only to silence it. We have here a good case in point; Edwards adds, in the tone of an aside, that Arminians find Calvinist doctrine 'to be wholly inconsistent with the sincerity of counsels, invitations, etc.' (p. 432) on the grounds that these 'invitations' imply beings who can *respond* or accept them and not only in the sense that God has elected them to do so. The problem, however, is soon passed and Edwards returns to his fortress; moral necessity does not excuse sin and, in any case, there is no freedom of the Arminian variety supposed to be necessary for justifying punishment for sin.

Edwards's next concern is to refute the Arminian objections to the doctrine of grace as both efficacious and irresistible. He states very clearly the substance of the Arminian claim, firm in the conviction that he has successfully answered it:

> The main objection of Arminians against this doctrine is, that it is inconsistent with their self-determining freedom of will; and that it is repugnant to the nature of virtue, that it should be wrought in the heart by the determining efficacy and power of another, instead of its being owing to a self-moving power; but in that case, the good which is wrought, would not be *our* virtue, but rather *God's* virtue

> . . . it has been demonstrated, that the liberty of moral agents does not consist in self-determining power; and that there is no need of any such liberty, in order to the nature of virtue; nor does it at all hinder, but that the state or act of the will may be the virtue of the subject, though it be not from self-determination, but the determination of an *extrinsic* cause . . . (p. 433, italics added)

In short, for Edwards the determination of moral necessity and providence prevail; although virtue may be attributed to the subject, it cannot be due to self-determination. Here Edwards invokes the premise on which his entire argument rests: There are not and cannot be any 'secondary' causes.

The emphasis placed by the Puritan tradition on the doctrine of predestination, the elect and the visible saints is well known; it forms the next focal point in Edwards's summary. His main concern here is with the alleged inconsistency between the *secret* and *revealed* will of God which is said to lead to the consequence that God is the author of sin. How, asked the Arminians, are we to reconcile the sincerity of God's precepts, calls, counsels, warnings and expostulations and the various means of grace which God uses to bring sinners to repentance with his absolute decree that only the elect are capable of responding? God's revealed will seems to address itself to all who can hear, while his secret will has already determined those who have been chosen. Edwards's reply is that God disposes all events and that he orders all things knowingly and by design; there is nothing new in the divine economy and all God's purposes are eternal:

> For if men are made true saints no otherwise than as God makes 'em so . . . and God thus makes some saints, and not others, on design or purpose, and no designs of God are new; it follows, that God thus distinguished from all others, all that ever become[6] true saints, by his eternal design or decree. (p. 435)

Accordingly, the secret and revealed will of God cannot be at odds.

The doctrine of election leads naturally to the question: For whom did Christ die? Arminians were especially concerned about Calvinist doctrine at this point, largely because of what we may call their 'universalism' and their denial that Christ died only for the elect. Christ died, says Edwards, 'in some sense' for all—to redeem 'visible Christians'; 'yea the whole world by his death'. Edwards, nevertheless, insists that 'there must be something *particular* in the design of his death', namely the actual salvation of the elect. Hence, the design for salvation by God is carried out for saving the elect and 'with respect to no other, most strictly speaking' (p. 435). It is interesting that at this point Edwards changes the emphasis dramatically away from what is particular in God's design to a general discussion about God's actually carrying out his purpose.

No doctrine was more disputed among Puritans both in England and America than the Calvinist notion of the perseverance of the saints. The question was: Can the true saints backslide and, as it were, 'fall from grace'? John Wesley for one made a great point of this question and wanted to know whether the failure of the saints to continue on the path of virtue might not be evidence that they were no true saints at all. Edwards's response to the question was two-fold; on the one hand, he spared no effort in trying to show that the doctrine of perseverance is found in 'all scripture'; on the other, he claimed that it is not the saints who persevere, but God who perseveres in them. This claim, he says, is supported by all he has established in the long argument of the *Freedom of the Will*: moral necessity and 'the infallible certainty of events' (p. 436) are not inconsistent with the virtue, or the rewards, commands, counsels and exhortations of God. This position is more uncompromising than the one Edwards set forth in the *Religious Affections*. There he was more sensitive to actual experience and was not working within the constraints of polemical discussion. In the earlier work, he took note of the weakness, moral failure and other shortcomings of the saints, insisting, nevertheless, that these are no more than aberrations that do not touch the foundations of the Spirit in the hearts of the elect.

Edwards's next to last word at the end of the *Freedom of the Will* is both typical and not a little disingenuous in the face of the supremely confident tone of the entire discussion—'But I must leave all these things to the consideration of the fair and impartial reader'. This is followed by a final statement that would have delighted Tertullian and would have drawn no objection from Kierkegaard:

> Indeed it is a glorious argument of the divinity of the holy Scriptures, that they teach such doctrines, which in one age or another, through the blindness of men's minds, and strong prejudices of their hearts, are rejected, as most absurd and unreasonable, by the wise and great men of the world. (p. 439)

Neither Tertullian nor Kierkegaard, however, would have been pleased with what Edwards went on to say about those scriptural doctrines—'which yet, when they are most carefully examined, appear to be exactly agreeable to the most demonstrable, certain, and natural dictates of reason'.

Having worked backwards, as it were from Edwards's final summary, we may now reverse direction and proceed to develop the main features of Edward's extended argument as it unfolds in his response to his opponents. In order to allow Edwards's position on so complex a topic to stand out as clearly as possible, the best approach is an expository one without critical interruptions that, however pertinent they may be, are more likely to confuse than enlighten a reader.

As in all other treatises, Edwards speaks on the basis of two sources —*biblical revelation* and *reason*, sometimes called understanding or common sense. On these two bases, Edwards aims to prove two principal theses: the first is that God's certain foreknowledge of all that happens, including human volitions, is utterly inconsistent with *contingency* anywhere in the world; the second is that the volitions of the human soul of Jesus were *necessarily* holy, and yet were subject to being called virtuous and praiseworthy. The first of these theses was directed against the belief in self-determination or freedom of the will which Edwards associated with the Arminian thinkers. The second was meant to refute the belief that what is necessitated cannot be the object of praise or blame. The entire argument of the *Freedom of the Will* is directed to the establishment of these two claims and, consequently, to the refutation of anti-Calvinist doctrine.

The discussion has both a theological and a philosophical dimension; the former has to do with the relation between the idea of freedom and the nature of God, while the latter focuses on the meaning of human agency, motive and volition in the defence of determinism. Edwards envisaged the theological issue in a simple and straightforward way: contingency, which in this context means essentially the 'liberty of self-determination', must be vanquished from the world. If it is not, God will be excluded from the whole of creation. For Edwards, there was no other alternative. Moreover, if anything were to come into existence, including volition, without a cause, the entire realm of morality and history would be totally disordered, with the result that God would be left with nothing to do but 'mend broken links as best he can'. By contrast, the philosophical aspect is far more complex, involving a detailed analysis of the determination of the will, the idea of the strongest motive, and the notions of necessity, impossibility, inability and contingency.

Before embarking on a discussion of the two theses noted above, it is necessary to understand Edwards's view of the moral situation, the meaning of will, of moral agency and of all that goes into the basis of volition. A word of caution is needed at this point. Edwards, like Berkeley, often contrasted the sense in which a word is 'generally understood' with meanings introduced by 'philosophers, metaphysicians and polemic divines' (p. 137), which, in Edwards's view, served to obscure things. It is, however, not to be supposed that he always regarded ordinary meaning as superior to those resulting from 'metaphysical refinement', because there are important places in his discussion where a philosophical or metaphysical meaning is called for and is used by Edwards along with a commonly accepted meaning drawn from ordinary discourse. If, moreover, Edwards finds that he can put the ordinary meaning of a term to good use, he tends to avail himself of the authority of the 'vulgar' meaning. Edwards has yet another way with words and that is to preface the meaning he attaches to a word or phrase with 'if the phrase be used with any meaning' (p. 141), thereby suggesting quite subtly that any other meaning is defective, if not devoid of any meaning at all. The problem facing the reader, especially in the case of *Freedom of the Will*, is to be clear about which practices Edwards is employing at a given stage of the argument.

'Will', Edwards says, '. . . is plainly, that by which the mind chooses anything . . . an act of will is the same as an act of choosing or choice' (p. 137). And by 'plainly' he means that no metaphysical considerations are involved. Choosing includes, for Edwards, refusing as well; and indeed he lists a great many pairs of options that fall within the scope of will—approving, disapproving, liking, disliking, embracing, rejecting, determining, directing, commanding, being pleased or displeased. 'All', he claims, 'may be reduced to this of choosing.' His view here follows the position he took in *Religious Affections*; to will is to be 'in some way inclined' as contrasted with being 'neutral' or merely contemplating the object in question. If there is any distinction between affections and will, it is in the former's being an inclination of the mind and heart, while the latter has to do with overt action. Will, for Edwards, is efficacious in the sense that God has made soul and body to be so united that the body always follows the choice made by the mind.

Edwards regarded will and desire as closely related and suggests that they might be distinguished insofar as will is always focused on what is present, while desire aims at what is absent. Edwards was, however, disinclined to follow Locke's tendency to equate will and desire because he believed that the two can and often do run counter to each other. One may *will* to persuade someone to follow a certain course of action, while at the same time *desiring* that the persuasion will not succeed.

Central to Edwards's analysis is the role of motive. Motive, he says, is the determining factor, but it has to be understood as a complex affair: 'It is that motive, which, as it stands in the view of the mind, is the strongest, that determines the will' (p. 141). Motive, for Edwards,

means the *whole* of the factors that lead to volition and the strength of that motive depends on that whole. The emphasis placed on 'in the view of the mind' is important because, for Edwards, what is not perceived 'can't affect the mind at all'. Here Edwards's organic and dynamic understanding of the self come into play. The life of the person is not a series of atomic events, but includes habits and tendencies that have been established over time. All motives, he says, have 'some sort and degree of tendency . . . previous to the effect . . . This previous tendency of the motive is what I call the "strength of motive" ' (p. 142). Unlike others who have regarded such motives as fame, wealth, happiness, and power as having a 'standard' strength without respect to the total make-up of the individual, Edwards insists that the determination of the strongest motive is a function of the previous advantage a motive has in moving the will. A person, for example, for whom fame or power has, in the view of the mind, no previous tendency to move the will, will regard them as weaker motives, by comparison with motives that do have that tendency.

Edwards takes it as 'without room for controversy' that 'whatever is perceived or apprehended by an intelligent and voluntary agent, which has the nature and influence of a motive to volition or choice, is considered or viewed *as good*' (p. 142). And, since whatever is so considered must appear eligible to the mind, 'the will always is as the greatest apparent good is'.[7] 'Good', says Edwards, means the same as 'agreeable', so that for something to appear good to the mind is the same as its appearing agreeable. Whatever has the greatest tendency to attract the mind is what *suits* the mind best and pleases it most. He makes a point of emphasizing that it is the 'direct and immediate object of the act of volition' which is in question, and not some remote or indirect feature connected with the object. In short, many acts of volition have remote relations to an object, but they are different from what is immediately willed and chosen. It is for this reason that Edwards always connected willing with the *present*, as we saw in his distinction between will and desire.

Edwards prefers his expression 'that the will always *is* as the greatest apparent good', to saying that the 'will is *determined* by the greatest apparent good' (p. 144) because he sees no clear distinction between what appears agreeable and suitable to the mind and the mind's preferring and choosing what so appears. According to Edwards, the 'will' is not some distinct entity that enters into the situation, but is the same as the mind's apprehension of the greatest apparent good. Having made clear this basic feature of volition, he devotes the remainder of the discussion in this section to considering what there is in the mind's view that leads it to regard an object as agreeable. Three factors are said to influence the mind's judgement—what appears in the object itself, the manner in which it is viewed, that is, the degree of firmness of assent with which the mind judges a future pleasure to be more or less probable, and the state of the mind that views the matter. In this third condition, Edwards was allowing for 'the particular temper which the mind has by nature' or which has been brought about by education, custom and example. Once again, Edwards is insisting on the involvement of the self as a whole in the determination of the greatest apparent good. It is for this reason that, in summing up his position, he agrees that the will always follows the last dictate of the understanding, if the understanding 'be taken in a large sense'—the *whole* faculty of apprehension.

Still working within the rubric of 'definition of terms', Edwards passes on to more complex matters—the meaning of necessity and contingency, the distinction between natural and moral necessity and the notion of liberty and moral agency. These ideas figure so largely in his total argument that he wanted to be as clear as possible in presenting his position before going on to deal directly with the first of the two principal theses noted above—whether there is any such freedom of the will which the Arminians regard as essential for all moral agents.

Edwards sets out to determine the meaning of necessity and impossibility by appealing first to what he regards as the ordinary meaning of the terms. We are not, he says, to express this meaning through such terms as 'must'—what is necessary 'must' be—and 'cannot'—what is impossible 'cannot' be—because these terms also need to be explained. Edwards, however, suggests that children use the ordinary words 'can', 'cannot', etc. and know something of what they mean before they meet the more technical terms. The main point he wants to make about the ordinary meaning of necessity is that it is 'relative' in the sense that there is always supposed some *opposition* to the existence of the thing; in the case of what is necessary, that opposition has been overcome.

Edwards's next distinction is between being necessary *in general*, by which he means things which are or will be notwithstanding any opposition from us, from others or from any quarter, and necessary *to us*, by which he means things which are and will be notwithstanding any opposition *from us*. Necessary, impossible and irresistible, he says, are essential to any discussion of moral agency when they are taken in the second sense. In summing up at this point, Edwards says that in the ordinary sense, 'A thing is said to be necessary, when we can't help it, let us do what we will' (p. 150). Similarly, something is impossible if we would do it, but find that our desires and endeavours are of no avail.

The reason for Edwards's excursion into ordinary meanings is not entirely clear, especially in view of the sequel in which he calls attention to the well-known fact that such meanings become so familiar and habitual that, when we come to assign technical meanings (Edwards calls them 'terms of art') to these same words, confusion results when we find ourselves falling back to the ordinary meanings. He seems to be concerned mainly to insist that the ordinary meanings of necessity and impossibility always suppose an opposition, so that anyone using them in cases that exclude opposition at the outset (for example, in the case of the divine necessity there is no opposition) is not using them 'in their proper signification' (p. 151).[8] No further appeal, however, is made to this signification at this point; instead, Edwards proceeds to define 'metaphysical' or 'philosophical' necessity as the key concept in his argument: 'Philosophical necessity is really nothing else than the full and fixed connection between the things signified by the subject and predicate of a proposition, which affirms something to be true' (p. 152). He prefaces this definition with the claim that the ground of the knowledge represented by the proposition 'is in things themselves'. The important point is that philosophical necessity is *independent* of whether any opposition or contrary effort is supposed. Edwards concludes: 'in this sense I use the word "necessity", in the following discourse, when I endeavor to prove that necessity is not inconsistent with liberty'.

The further elucidation of the three ways in which the subject and predicate of a proposition may have a certain or necessary connection is illuminating in that these ways reveal all the hallmarks of the determinist position. First, the connection between the two terms may be 'in and of' themselves, because to suppose that they are not connected may be contradictory or absurd. For Edwards, the eternal existence of being generally falls into this category, along with the attributes of God and 'innumerable metaphysical and mathematical truths'. The second way is less clear because more emphasis is placed on the *truth* of the proposition involved. The proposition affirming the existence of something may be fixed and certain because the existence of that thing has already come to pass, so that this proposition becomes certain and unalterably true; the past event 'has fixed and decided the matter', so that it is impossible that existence not be predicated of it. From this Edwards concludes, 'the existence of whatever is already come to pass, is now become necessary', since it cannot be other than true that such a thing has happened.

Edwards's conflation of the truth that what has already happened is now certain with the past becoming 'necessary' is to be explained by the third way according to which the connection may be *consequential*. The point here is that whatever is perfectly connected with what is necessary, itself becomes necessary. It is only in this way, he says, that what is future becomes necessary; not because it is necessary in itself nor that it becomes necessary by already coming to pass, but only because the future has become connected with something that is necessary. The sentence that expresses this quite important contention is not without ambiguity:

> . . . the only way that anything that is to come to pass hereafter, is or can be necessary, is by a connection with something that is necessary in its own nature, or something that already is, or has been; so that the one being supposed, the other certainly follows.

It would seem that the *necessity* of all that is to happen, according to this view, would have to stem either from God or from the past or from both, depending on where the emphasis falls, since, in any case, God is the ground of the necessity attaching to all that has been. Finally, Edwards adds, 'this is the necessity which especially belongs to controversies about the acts of the will' (p. 154).

In two short paragraphs he deals with the meaning of 'contingent', and this is a place where the 'common signification' of the term takes *precedence* over the use of the term 'by polemic writers' who diverge from this ordinary meaning. According to Edwards, the ordinary meaning of contingent is anything that comes to pass by chance or accident so that its connection with the established course of things 'is not discerned' and there can be no foresight. By contrast, polemic writers use the term in a quite different sense, namely, for something that has no previous ground or reason with which its existence has any fixed connection. Needless to say, this is not the sense in which Edwards uses the term.

Edwards laid great store by the distinction between 'moral' and 'natural' necessity and it figures essentially in his efforts to refute his opponents. After citing several senses in which we speak of moral necessity—being under moral obligation, the apparent connection of things as distinct from absolute necessity which is said to be much the same as that high degree of probability which is ordinarily sufficient for our behaviour in the world—Edwards sets forth what he means by the expression and how it will be used in the 'following discourse'. Moral necessity is 'that necessity of connection and consequence, which arises from such *moral causes*, as the strength of inclination, or motives, and the connection which there is in many cases between these, and such certain volitions and actions' (p. 156).

By natural necessity, Edwards means being under the necessity of natural causes; under certain circumstances we necessarily have sensations, feel pain, see objects, fall downwards when our bodies have no support. Interestingly enough, he includes among these causes assent to the truth of certain propositions as soon as the terms are understood, as that two and two make four. All of this is to be distinguished from moral causes, habits and dispositions.

The central contention of his argument regarding the determination of the will is that moral necessity may be as absolute as natural necessity and that there may be such a thing 'as a sure and perfect connection between moral causes and effects'. This connection, Edwards says, is what he expressly means by moral necessity. To make the meaning clearer, Edwards goes on to point out that the nature of things is as much involved in moral necessity as in natural necessity. The difference between the two is not found in the nature of the connection, but rather in the nature of the terms connected. When moral necessity is in question, the cause is of a moral nature—some previous disposition or some motive in view of the understanding—and the effect is also of a moral nature—a volition of the soul or a voluntary action. At this point we must recall what was said above about the difference between what necessity means in common speech and its philosophical meaning. The former always supposes some voluntary opposition or endeavour, while the latter does not. Moral necessity draws for its meaning on the philosophical sense and thus, says Edwards, no opposition can be involved because moral necessity is a certainty of the will itself: 'For 'tis absurd to suppose the same individual will to oppose itself, in its present act'—an absurdity that is said to be the same as to talk of two contrary motions in the same moving body at the same time.

In short, for Edwards there is no conflict *within* the will because the will *is* as the greatest apparent good is, and the connection between the two is what constitutes moral necessity. An important consequence of this idea is that Edwards brings together all features of moral agency in *willing*. It is incorrect to say, Edwards writes, 'that a person can't perform those external actions . . . which would be easily performed, if the act of the will were present'. The reason is that 'it is easy for the man to do the thing if he will, but the very willing is the doing; when once he has willed, the thing is performed; and nothing else remains to be done' (p. 162).[9] Hence we are not to talk of being *able*, but of being *willing*.

The final notions Edwards saw fit to deal with before launching his attack on the Arminian conception of freedom are the ideas of liberty and moral agency. The reader will have no difficulty in seeing that what Edwards has to say about these two ideas determines his entire argument against what he takes to be the Arminian notion of liberty as 'consisting in the will's self-determining power'. Liberty, says

Edwards, means 'in common speech' (p. 171) the opportunity or advantage to do as one pleases in the absence of any hindrance, and the opposite of liberty is the presence of obstacles that make it impossible for the individual to accomplish what he wills. Liberty can be ascribed to no being that has not a will, and from this Edwards concludes that to speak of liberty as belonging to the *will* 'is not to speak good sense'. Here Edwards invokes the authority of the 'original and proper significance of words' (p. 163). Accordingly, he says, 'the will is not an agent that has a will', because 'that which has the power of volition . . . is the man or the soul, and not the power of volition itself' (p. 163).

Here we confront the ambiguity noted previously: Is it the freedom of the person, or the freedom of the will that is at stake? Edwards stresses the freedom of the person at this point in order to address the freedom of the 'will' conception focused by the Arminians. His argument, as we shall see, will be to invoke the infinite regress; if the will has a 'will', that will must also have a will, and the process will be unending as it stretches backwards in time. By insisting on the idea that liberty means that there is nothing standing in the way—'the common and primary notion of freedom'—Edwards is able to claim that freedom is not incompatible with the individual's necessarily willing what he or she can will in accordance with a nature or self already determined apart from any choice about that nature or self.

In pressing this point against the Arminians, Edwards claims that they use the term 'liberty' in a sense that violates the common meaning. He cites three considerations: first, that they introduce the idea of a self-determining will that is supposed to be independent of any prior conditions; secondly, that they appeal to indifference or a will that is initially *in equilibrio* (which, of course, is, on Edwards's view, no will at all, since will *is* a choice); thirdly, that they appeal to contingency, which he has already defined as an event disconnected from all fixed relations to the course of events. In a crucial sentence Edwards makes his main point against his opponents: 'They suppose the essence of liberty so much to consist in these things [the three previous considerations], that unless the will of man be free in this sense, he has no real freedom, how much soever he may be at liberty to act according to his will' (p. 165). The long discussion that follows about the 'will's determining itself' as being essential to human freedom, depends entirely on the two points Edwards set forth in his analysis of terms; liberty means nothing else than the ability to will without hindrance, and will is a property of the self or the agent and not a property of the will.

In typical fashion, Edwards seeks to consolidate his point by a comparison of man with God. God, he says, is never a subject as man clearly is, and hence God is not under the sway of rules and conditions, but acts entirely from his own nature. Such a mode of action is the paradigm for man since man is made in the image of God. What this means is that man *must* do as he wills, in accordance with the fallen nature that he has and he has liberty only in the sense that there is nothing preventing him from doing what he wills in accordance with his own nature.

Having thus prepared the way, Edwards sets out to show the 'manifest inconsistencies' in the Arminian doctrine of freedom. Here Edwards repeats the point he has made so often, namely, that actions are to be ascribed to agents and not to the powers of agents, and hence there is some impropriety in speaking about the *will* determining the will. In all cases, he says, we can only mean that it is the agent who exercises the power of willing. When we say, for example, that valour fights courageously or that love seeks the object loved, we mean that the man fights courageously and seeks the object loved. Hence, if Arminians insist on the 'will's determining itself', they can only mean that it is the agent who is making the decisions. In any case, says Edwards, there is a contradiction in the entire notion because preceding *every* free act there must be another free act and so on, with the consequence that there must be 'an act of the will preceding the first act in the whole train' (p. 172)—a free act of the will before the first free act of the will. Since we are caught in an infinite regress, Edwards contends that we must come finally to an act of the will determining all that follows which is *not* a free act. And if this purported first act is not free, 'none of them all can be free'. Edwards concludes that this notion of freedom is incoherent.

Edwards's strategy is quite simple; he wants to insist that no events, and human actions in particular, come about without a cause, and at the same time he aims at exposing the view of his opponents by claiming that their conception of freedom means actions that are without any cause. By a cause Edwards understands not only what has 'positive efficacy'—the notion of efficient cause—but any conditions that serve as a ground or reason why certain events take place and not otherwise. The sun, he says, is the cause of the 'ascending of the vapors in the daytime' but the absence of the sun in the night is not the cause, in the same sense, of the falling of the dew. Yet the absence of the sun is an *antecedent* to the condensation of the moisture and thus counts as a cause. In addition, cause will mean moral cause as well as natural cause, and the former is as real as the latter. In a passage that echoes the cosmological argument for God's existence, Edwards declares that what is self-existent is from eternity and unchanging, while whatever *begins to be* must have some foundation of existence from outside itself. If, Edwards says, 'this grand principle of common sense' be taken away, there can be no arguing from effects to their causes; whatever is not necessary in itself must have a cause. He even goes so far as to claim that if this principle is denied, we should have no proof of the being of God and no guarantee of the existence of anything beyond our own immediate ideas. All of this is meant to count decisively against the idea that there are acts of will coming to pass without a cause.[10]

The complexity of Edwards's argument against the Arminians notwithstanding, the force of his claim is quite simple. All causal connections are *necessary* connections and the connections between moral causes or motives and the acts that follow are as necessarily connected as the falling of the body to the ground if it has no support. The notion of contingency is abolished for, says Edwards, to suppose that there are events that do have a cause or ground of existence and are not *necessarily* connected with that cause, 'is to suppose that they have a cause that is not their cause' (p. 215). The force of the denial of contingency in the world becomes evident when Edwards comes to the divine foreknowledge—the underlying reason for his defence of determinism in all human volition.

The stage is now set for Edwards to pursue the two theses noted above: first, that God's certain foreknowledge of all that happens, including human volition, is utterly inconsistent with *contingency* anywhere in the world, and, secondly, that the volition of the human soul of Jesus was *necessarily* holy and yet subject to being called virtuous and praiseworthy. Edwards begins by calling attention to what he had said previously about the meaning of necessity. Whatever is connected firmly with what is necessary, is itself necessary. The divine foreknowledge is a thing 'which already *has*, and long ago *had* existence' and thus it is utterly impossible for it to be otherwise. The future existence of all the volitions of moral agents is infallibly connected with that foreknowledge and, since the foreknowledge is necessary, all actions are themselves necessary. It would be a contradiction, Edwards contends, to say that something firmly connected with what is necessary, may '*possibly not exist*'. In short, the only 'possibility' before the fact which can be considered at all, is the *one* possibility that had to happen or was necessary. Foreknowledge eliminates the possibility of contingency in the world, for contingency is the antithesis of God's unlimited prescience.

In the course of the argument (Part II, sections 11, 12), Edwards appeals to a mutual implication of foreknowledge and necessity. When he takes foreknowledge as a fact established in Scripture, his claim is that without necessity in all things, that foreknowledge would not be possible and such a consequence is not to be allowed. When he starts with the philosophical theory of necessity in the nature of things, his claim is that the necessary being must have foreknowledge of all events and human volitions. Edwards presents a formidable mass of examples from the Bible to support the fact of God's foreknowledge, and he prefaces the discussion by saying that it should not be necessary to prove the point since it is contained in Scripture and that is always true. However, he continues, there are those who claim to accept Scripture, but entertain doubts about foreknowledge, and hence he must lay the matter out. Edwards cites two axioms concerning God's predictions of future events; first, to foretell is to profess to foreknow; secondly, God's foreknowledge of future volitions includes what is consequent to them and dependent upon them.

When Moses was in Egypt, God foretold the Pharaoh's future disobedience in his refusal to let the people go. He foretold the moral conduct of Josiah (1 Kings 13:1–6, 32) 'three hundred years before he was born'. God foretold the sin of Peter, not only the act but the consequences as well. God foretold to Abraham that the people of Israel would go down to Egypt. God's prescience, says Edwards, is not confined to individuals, but extends to the future conduct of nations and peoples. Thus God foretold that the Jews would return from the Babylonian captivity and he indicated all the persecutions that would be visited on St Paul. God, moreover, foretold the Antichrist, the Man of Sin, and all the consequences that would follow. Reversing the order, Edwards argues that unless God had foreknowledge he would be ignorant of what was promised about the Kingdom of God, and indeed all of prophecy would have no basis in the divine foreknowledge if God did not know the future volitions of man. As a summary, Edwards cites the words of James (Acts 15:18): 'Known unto God are all his works from the beginning of the world', and claims that this statement would have to be false unless God had foreknowledge. Even more, if God were ignorant of the future, he would find himself repenting and changing his mind, all of which does not happen. Finally, without foreknowledge, God would be frustrated in realizing the end for which he created the world, something that is contrary to all Scripture.

One of the arguments—Edwards calls them 'evasions'—of his opponents about the matter of foreknowledge caused him special concern, namely, the use of the distinction between God's foreknowledge and his decrees. Whitby, in his *Discourse on the Five Points* (1710), cited Origen's statement, 'God's prescience is not the cause of things future, but their being future is the cause of God's prescience that they will be' (pp. 262–3). The idea is that while foreknowledge may prove the necessity of what is foreknown, it need not be the *cause* of that necessity since the latter is established by the divine decree. For Edwards, this is a mistake because it assumes that nothing can be evidence of a thing's being necessary except what has a causal influence on it. Edwards's claim is that if foreknowledge is not what first *makes* it impossible for the future to be otherwise, it does *demonstrate* the impossibility in whatever way it comes about: 'If foreknowledge be not the cause but the effect of that impossibility, it may prove that there is such an impossibility, as much as if it were the cause' (p. 264). An argument from effect to cause, he says, can be as strong as one from cause to effect. Edwards's point is that it is impossible that what is infallibly known to be true should be otherwise, whether the knowledge be the cause of the necessity or vice versa.

As always, Edwards appeals to the certainty in things themselves as the ground of all knowledge and hence he can agree with Whitby 'that mere knowledge don't affect the thing known' (p. 265). The admission, however, is not damaging in Edwards's view because 'a *certain knowledge* of futurity, supposes *certain futurity*, antecedent to that certain knowledge'. Those who say that God's foreknowledge is not the cause but the effect of the foreknown event are, says Edwards, arguing against themselves. Why is this so? The answer is found in Edwards's idea that in foreknowledge the existence of the event is so firm 'that it is as if it had already been; inasmuch as *in effect* it actually exists already, its future existence has already had actual influence . . . and has produced an effect, viz. prescience' (p. 265).

Edwards's argument may be more difficult to comprehend at the present time than was true in the heyday of Newtonian determinism. The new emphasis on the reality of time means that there is a *real* future that has not yet come to pass and which is future in at least some of its features—even for God. Edwards's entire argument depends, like that of all determinisms, on abolishing time, because in God everything is 'all there' at once—*totum simul*—and this includes the future no less than the past. Since the future is *present* to God, it can have its efficacy because 'in effect' it exists already, and thus can be the cause of divine foreknowledge. Edwards states this view in several remarkably clear and unambiguous sentences: 'future events are always in God's view as evident, clear, sure and necessary, as if they already were' (p. 267). God's knowledge, being absolutely perfect, is 'without succession', hence 'all things, whether past, present or to come', are 'viewed with the equal evidence and fullness; future things being seen with as much clearness, as if they were present' (p. 268).

Edwards's final barb against his opponents is that Calvinist doctrine about the divine decrees does not involve 'any more fatality in things' than is implied in the acknowledgement by Arminians of God's omniscience and universal prescience. Therefore, he concludes, 'all objections they make against the doctrine of the Calvinists, as implying Hobbes' doctrine of necessity, or the Stoical doctrine of fate, lie no more against the doctrine of Calvinists, than their own doctrine' (p. 269). Edwards appealed to this parity in views when he had to respond to the standard charge of the Arminians that in Calvinism God is the author of sin. Free will, he insisted, is no more effective in dispelling this disquieting consequence than is predestination, and Edwards is content to say that this is 'a difficulty wherein the Arminians share with us'.[11]

Edwards had still another arrow in his quiver and he aimed it squarely against Isaac Watts's *Essay on the Freedom of Will*.[12] Drawing again on his contention that all causal connections are necessary, Edwards sets out to show an incoherence in Watts's view that necessity is inconsistent with liberty. If acts of the will are not necessary, says Edwards, they can come about only by chance, but Watts asserts that 'chance can never be properly applied to the acts of the will' (p. 271). Edwards's response is that therefore they can only be necessary. In short, according to Edwards, the Arminian notion of liberty includes contingency, but contingency is inconsistent with that notion because Arminians themselves claim that all willing is by *design* and not chance. For Edwards, the antithesis is complete and unavoidable: either human volition takes place under necessity, or we shall be given up to a wild contingency, 'liable to act unintelligently and unreasonably' (p. 273).

Edwards's next task is to destroy the idea that necessary volitions cannot be regarded as virtuous nor can they be subject to praise and blame. The focus of his attack is Whitby's *Discourse* containing the thesis that freedom from necessity is a condition for ascribing virtue or vice, praise or blame, reward or punishment. Edwards's strategy is to use the moral conduct of the human soul of Christ as the paradigm for volition that is necessarily holy, but still subject to being called virtuous and praiseworthy. His central thesis is that the acts of Christ could not have been otherwise than holy or agreeable to God's will, and he cites no less than eleven reasons for this contention. These may be conflated since they all depend on the divine promises and the realization of God's ultimate purpose in creation. God promised to preserve Christ from yielding to temptations that would have negated his role in the divine economy; God made promises to the Messiah for the success of his office as mediator; God promised the Church of the Old Testament that a sinless saviour would be forthcoming; all these promises would have been nullified if it were possible that Christ should fall into sin. Despite the necessity of his conduct, however, Edwards insists that the holiness of Jesus was praiseworthy and deserving of merit, as is to be seen when God speaks of being well pleased with the righteousness of his servant and finds his obedience more acceptable than the sacrifices of old.

Although Edwards pursues the point at great length in opposition to Whitby and argues on philosophical and theological grounds that the necessary inability of fallen man to act otherwise than he does is compatible with his being blameworthy, he sets this aside in order to show that 'common sense' and the 'natural notions of mankind' support his position. In a remarkably short paragraph, Edwards claims that, if all ambiguities and philosophical subtleties are set aside, the natural apprehensions of mankind show that what is *morally* necessary is nevertheless thought to be subject to praise and blame, reward and punishment. Starting with the common notion of faultiness, Edwards writes:

> The idea which the common people through all ages and nations have of faultiness, I suppose to be plainly this: a person's being or doing wrong, with his own will and pleasure; containing these two things: 1. His doing wrong, when he does as he pleases. 2. His pleasure's being wrong. Or in other words . . . a person's having his heart wrong, and doing wrong from his heart. And this is the sum total of the matter. (p. 357)

The common people, says Edwards, do not pay attention to metaphysical abstractions in order to form their notion of what is blameworthy, nor do they wait until they know what determines the will, whether it be intrinsic or extrinsic, whether the will or the understanding determines the will, etc. If it were necessary to resort to metaphysics in the first instance, the vast majority of people would have no idea of what it means to be at fault. On the contrary, Edwards says, even children have some sense of *desert* long before they have heard of any philosophical ideas, and this stems from *experience* and a *natural sensation* of fitness in connecting moral evil with being or doing wrong with the will. Edwards calls this natural sense by the name of 'conscience'. The common people, moreover, do understand that a faulty deed is to be regarded as a person's *own deed*, but they do not understand this to mean that some motion must *begin of itself* or come about *accidentally*. In short, the ordinary notion excludes what Edwards took to be the main contentions of the Arminians.

The common people do think that a faulty or praiseworthy deed is done in the exercise of *liberty*, but, once again according to Edwards, by liberty they mean only that the person can do as he pleases and they know nothing of the will's causing its own acts, or determining itself, or indeed of 'any confused metaphysical speculation' (p. 359). The next, and crucial, point in Edwards's excursion into determining ordinary meanings is the belief that the more necessarily the act is connected with the person's propensity to good, the more praiseworthy is that act. Edwards's contention here was expressed many years later and in a far more elegant style by F.H. Bradley in his *Ethical Studies* (1876) when he was considering the 'vulgar notion of responsibility'. Using a different idiom, Bradley maintained that we do not object to the *prediction*—the model of determinism—of our conduct when it has to do with an act that is thought to stem *necessarily* from our established character. On the contrary, one is honoured when it is said 'We *know* that Jones would not, could not, will not, betray his trust', because this is a recognition of a praiseworthy person. Edwards says the same thing in his ponderous prose:

> If there be an approach to a moral necessity in a man's exertion of good acts of will, they being the exercise of a strong propensity to good, and a very powerful love to virtue; 'tis far from being the dictate of common sense, that he is less virtuous, and the less to be esteemed, loved and praised; that 'tis agreeable to the natural notions of all mankind that he is so much the better man, worthy of greater respect, and higher commendation. (p. 360)

The difference, however, between the two is that Bradley's man will have something to say about the formation of the character that is to do the determining, while Edwards's man will have inherited that character entirely from beyond his own capacities. We are back again to the issue posed at the outset: Is it the freedom of the man, or the freedom of the will that is at stake?

Edwards might have dealt in more depth with the first freedom—what part does freedom play in the formation of the human *character*?—if he had been less concerned to dwell exclusively on his deterministic argument against the proponents of the freedom of the 'will'. What Edwards did not see is that the Arminians, and I suppose that we must count Bradley among them, could admit and even insist upon the sort of determinism according to character cited by Edwards, but with the proviso that Jones might *not* have remained true to character in the predicated case and might have done otherwise. To put it crudely, the Arminians thought it a 'credit' to the person to *continue to will* that good character when there was still a *possibility* not to do so as seems plainly indicated by actual experience.

An excellent example of what Edwards would have to call moral necessity is found in the famous words of Martin Luther at the Diet of

Worms. 'Here I stand', he said, 'I can do no other.' It is obvious that he could have done other, but he could not have done so and still remained the moral personality known as Martin Luther. In short, *being* Martin Luther meant that he could do no other. Edwards would interpret this, not as a manifestation of the freedom of the Christian *man* as Luther did, but as the act of God in Luther. All depends, for Edwards, on his belief that to admit any secondary causes means the denial of the divine sovereignty. Edwards, in the end, for all of his emphasis on ordinary meaning, saw the entire spectrum of moral endeavour solely in terms of his model of the visible saints whose character is already determinate. This emphasis became particularly apparent when he had to deal with the problem of 'backsliding'—can the saints ever fail to continue to will their holy character?

Edwards, nevertheless, now had all he needed to defeat his opponents; he had only to apply, admittedly on a more sophisticated level, these deliverances of common sense in order to criticize the Arminian doctrines. It is important to take note of the great authority Edwards attaches here to these 'natural notions of mankind'. His claim is that, according to these notions, moral necessity is perfectly *consistent* with the ascribing of praise and blame to human actions. Hence, if the Arminians believe that they base their views on common sense, they are mistaken. And, even more, says Edwards, they are under the illusion that they argue from common sense when in fact they use such terms as 'liberty', 'necessity', and 'impossible' in a *metaphysical* sense that deviates from their 'original and vulgar sense'. In going against common sense, the Arminians were also nullifying the 'universal dictates of the reason of mankind'. In the compounding of reason and common sense with the ordinary meaning of certain basic terms, Edwards appears to be making a double claim. On its weaker side, the charge is that ordinary meanings do not support the Arminian position, and hence that its proponents can lay no claim to be basing their position on these meanings. On its stronger side, the charge is that, in perverting these meanings, the Arminians resort to metaphysical notions that are *wrong* in virtue of the fact that they are inconsistent with the ordinary meanings that represent the voice of reason.[13]

Edwards throws further light on this matter in a section in *Freedom of the Will* which comes just prior to the 'Conclusion' with which this chapter began. In this section, Edwards is defending himself and 'Calvinistic doctrine' against the charge that it is supported 'by abstruse metaphysical subtleties' (p. 423) set in opposition to common sense. He begins by admitting that it is possible to make such a charge against his arguments, but he counters at once with the claim that metaphysics is needed in order, for example, to understand the nature and being of God, of mathematics and of the course of things in the world. But, he continues, it is no valid objection to a line of reasoning to call it 'metaphysical' because the real question is whether the reasoning be good and the arguments conclusive. It is as illegitimate, says Edwards, to refute someone by calling his arguments 'metaphysical', as it would be to tell someone that his arguments are insubstantial because they were written in Latin, French, English or Mohawk.

It is clear that Edwards had no intention of dispensing with metaphysics, nor will he admit that it need be 'abstruse, unintelligible and akin to the jargon of the schools' (p. 424). He sees his own extended argument as the casting in a precise and disciplined way of what is founded in experience and reason. There is, he says, 'no high degree of refinement and abstruse speculation' in determining—and then follows the main points he has made against the Arminians—that a thing can't be before itself and hence cannot be its own cause; that an act of free choice can't have an act of free choice before it; that nothing can begin to be without a cause, etc. All of this he takes to be 'plain' and without sophistry.

Finally, Edwards states the underlying reason for the entire discussion about the relation between common sense and metaphysics: he wants to turn the tables against the Arminians. The following statement makes this clear and unambiguous:

> 'Tis far from being true . . . that the proof of the doctrine which has been maintained, depends on certain abstruse, unintelligible, metaphysical terms and notions; and that the Arminian scheme, without needing such clouds and darkness, for its defense, is supported by the plain dictates of common sense; that the very reverse is most certainly true, and that to a great degree. (p. 428)

In short, Edwards's metaphysics has the support of common sense, while his opponents not only have no such support for their position, but it is vitiated as well by a false metaphysics.

Notes

1 This is the title of Part II, section 1 in the text.

2 See Paul Ramsey's Introduction to *Freedom of the Will, The Works of Jonathan Edwards* 1 (New Haven: Yale University Press, 1957), 'Edwards and his Antagonists', pp. 65ff. The texts cited by Edwards are: Thomas Chubb, *Tracts* (1730); Daniel Whitby, *Discourse on the Five Points* (1710)—this is Edwards's short title for the original ten-line title which recites the famous five points of Calvinism announced by the Synod of Dort in 1619 and previously by the Arminian Remonstrance in 1610—and

Isaac Watts, whom Edwards does not name but refers to him as 'the author of *An Essay on the Freedom of Will in God and the Creature*'. It is important to bear in mind, as Ramsey notes, that while these three thinkers are associated polemically by Edwards, they represent a diversity of backgrounds and opinions. Chubb is generally regarded as a Deist; Whitby was a minister of the Church of England, and Watts was a dissenting minister in Edwards's own tradition.

3 Readers should consult Paul Ramsey's Introduction, where he defines the situation in his comment that ' "Arminianism" became but a loose term for all forms of the complaint of the aggrieved moral nature against the harsh tenets of Calvinism'. Page references in the text are to this edition.

4 The full title is '*A Careful and Strict Enquiry* into the *modern* prevailing Notions of that Freedom of Will which is supposed to be essential to Moral Agency, Virtue and Vice, Reward and Punishment, Praise and Blame'. The use of a short title scarcely needs defence, especially when the full title is a thesis in its own right.

5 See below where Edwards admits that Christ died to save the world, but insists that there had to be something 'particular' in his death—the salvation of the elect.

6 One of the oversights of all determinisms has to do with what can possibly be meant by 'becoming'. All that can be meant is that there is some sort of disclosure of what was 'already there'. Thus, on Edwards's view, we cannot speak of someone 'becoming' a saint, since that person *always was* a saint, and the 'becoming' can mean no more than a revealing in time what had already become. See Perry Miller's comment that Edwards saw that the Calvinists were no better than the Arminians at keeping God from being the author of sin. Perry Miller, *Jonathan Edwards* (New York: William Sloane Associates, 1949), p. 259.

7 'Apparent good' must be understood as a judgement or estimate of an object or act as all the factors 'appear' before the mind. 'Apparent' does not mean merely 'appears' to be good in contrast to being 'really' good, since the implied contrast between appearance and reality is not involved.

8 It is possible that what Edwards means, although he does not say so explicitly, is that those using the terms in question in cases where no opposition is involved cannot be using them in the ordinary sense, but are using them in a *philosophical* sense for which they cannot claim the support of ordinary use.

9 This idealistic conflation of 'willing'—for Edwards always 'choosing'—and performing, or actually doing, has an exact modern counterpart in the aesthetic theory of Benedetto Croce (1866–1952). Croce held that as soon as the artist has the conception of the artistic work, the work has been accomplished.

10 It is important to notice that Edwards does not normally avail himself of a cosmological argument for God's existence—he is too completely involved in an ontological approach—but he is not opposed to citing the damage that would be done to such an argument if the causal principle were to be denied.

11 In his explicit treatment of the question, Is God the author of sin? (Part IC, section 9), Edwards writes: 'if there be any difficulty in this matter, 'tis nothing peculiar to this scheme [Edwards's position]; 'tis no difficulty or disadvantage wherein it is distinguished from the scheme of Arminians . . .'. If, Edwards continues, God is the author of all that happens, including the existence of sin, 'this is a difficulty which equally attends the doctrine of Arminians themselves; at least of those of them that allow God's certain foreknowledge'.

12 This essay was published (London, 1732) bound with another one, but with no author's name on the title page; it was subsequently included in a collection of Watts's writings (1752). Edwards cautiously does not name Watts, referring only to 'the author'.

13 Berkeley, as is well known, appealed to the authority of ordinary meanings—'I side in all things with the mob'—as the measure of 'metaphysical abstractions' and Edwards is doing the same thing. This approach made its appearance in force in the 'ordinary language' philosophers of the early part of this century of which G. E. Moore would be an example. He was, however, somewhat more circumspect about the authority of such language. I am aware that there has been much dispute about Moore's view on the point, but having attended several of his seminars held at Columbia University in the early 1940s, I am confident that he meant to stress two points: first, that if a philosopher uses words—in his own words—'in a sense in which no one ever uses them', there is *prima facie* reason for doubting the validity of what he says; secondly, deviation from ordinary meaning does not *ipso facto* condemn a position as false without further discussion. In the text above, Edwards is claiming that deviation from ordinary meanings not only deprives Arminians of the support of common sense, but also renders their metaphysical notions false.

5

The doctrine of original sin

The Great Christian Doctrine of Original Sin Defended[1] first appeared in 1758 and the original title page tells its own story: 'By the late Reverend and learned JONATHAN EDWARDS, A. M. President of the College of New Jersey'. Edwards had died of smallpox earlier in that year, shortly after he had accepted the Presidency of the College, now Princeton University. *Original Sin* was not only a substantial contribution to the controversy over the doctrine that took place among theologians, but it also played its part in the larger debate between the Enlightenment belief in the innate goodness of the natural man and the emphasis placed by the Reformation on human depravity.[2] While Edwards's discussion of the issues focuses largely on the theological controversy—especially in connection with his polemic against John Taylor—it is clear that he was greatly concerned about the spread of Enlightenment conceptions of the nature of man since for the most part they ran counter to Calvinist doctrine.

Original Sin, like the *Freedom of the Will*, has a formal 'Conclusion' at the end, but there the similarity ends. In the *Will*, Edwards provided a summary of his main contentions, but here he does nothing of the sort and focuses instead on the matter of biblical interpretation, the only topic mentioned. In view of this fact, it is important to take note of the special point he was making. Much of Edwards's argument in *Original Sin* is directed against Taylor's *Scripture-Doctrine of Original Sin*, but now Edwards voices a different concern: 'I observe there are some *other* things, besides arguments, in Dr. Taylor's book' (p. 434), which are intended to influence the minds of readers, especially, in Edwards's view, simple readers. What Edwards means by the 'other things' are what he calls the use of 'artful methods' by Taylor and 'many of the late opposers of the more peculiar doctrines of Christianity' for the purpose of nullifying the effect of the 'clearest Scripture evidences, in favor of those important doctrines' (p. 434). These methods, says Edwards, are aimed at making 'void the arguments taken from the writings of the Apostle Paul, in which those doctrines are more plainly and fully revealed, than in any other part of the Bible'. In his typical fashion, Edwards introduces a point in a somewhat cryptic way and then finally adds 'What I mean is this . . .'.

Edwards's charge is that his opponents express a high opinion of Paul and speak of him as a masterly writer with extensive reach and deep design, but that these expressions are *specious*. They carry a plausible appearance of Christian zeal and attachment to the Scriptures, but Edwards is convinced that behind the appearance lies the aim to 'make way for the reception of their own peculiar sentiments' (p. 435). The incautious reader may be deceived and come to think that he or she has not rightly understood much of the Apostle's writings, 'which before seemed very plain to men' (p. 435), and thus come to look favourably on the *interpretations* put upon the words of Paul by 'these *new writers*'. Edwards's contention is that these new interpretations involve meanings which 'before lay entirely out of sight' and appear to be quite foreign to both what the common reader takes to be their obvious sense, and the expositions of the best commentators.

In an ironic passage that matches Nietzsche at his best, Edwards goes on to say that, of course, the depth of Paul's thought was beyond the capacities of learned divines, the preachers and expositors of the Reformation, and even the members of the Westminster Assembly! There is, however, a remedy; Edwards's response is worth quoting in full:

> It must be understood, that there is risen up, now at length in this happy age of life and liberty, a set of men, of a more free and generous turn of mind, a more inquisitive genius, and better discernment. By such insinuations, they seek advantage to their cause; and thus the most unreasonable and extravagant interpretations of Scripture are palliated and recommended . . .[3]

It is clear that Edwards's great concern here with biblical interpretation stems from the emphasis placed by Taylor, especially, on the *scriptural* basis of his position on original sin. Whatever may be the case with philosophical or even general theological matters, Edwards had the greatest confidence in his knowledge of biblical exegesis.[4] One example will suffice to make the point; it shows at the same time that Edwards made such uncompromising demands upon his opponents as to amount to overkill on his part and even to border on the pedantic.

The occasion is Edwards's 'Remarks on Dr. Taylor's way of explaining this text [Romans 5:12 to the end]'[5]. Edwards does not quote the text itself; the following is the verse in the King James version: 'Wherefore, as by one man sin entered into the world, and death by sin; and so death passed upon all men, for that all have sinned'. Edwards fastens on the meaning of 'death' in this verse and in succeeding ones. We need not follow the whole discussion in order to give a clear indication of Edwards's approach. According to Edwards, Taylor insists that 'by death in this place no more is meant, than that death which we all die, when this present life is extinguished', and that this meaning persists in verses 14, 15, and 17. Edwards claims that Taylor 'speaks of it as evidently, clearly and infallibly so . . . that the Apostle means no more by death, throughout this paragraph'. But, says Edwards, what Taylor writes elsewhere shows that there is nothing 'infallible' about his pronouncement, since in commenting on 'The wages of sin is death; but the gift of God is eternal life . . .' (Rom 6:23) Taylor writes 'Death in this place is widely different from the death we now die; as it stands there opposed to eternal life'.

Taylor, it is clear, is aware of both the meanings assigned to 'death', but in Edwards's view Taylor is guilty of declaring 'infallibly' that the first meaning of death is the only one involved and then going on to admit the existence of the second meaning.[6] Here, Edwards concludes, 'is manifest proof, against infallible evidence!' Edwards is, of course, supposing that Taylor's 'certainty' about the reference to temporal death in Romans 5:12 must somehow prevent him from recognizing that there is in Paul's thought the second meaning as well. Or, even worse, if Taylor acknowledges the meaning that death has in contrast to eternal life, he is contradicting himself. Surely, this is an exaggeration on Edwards's part, but it is typical of his treatment of opponents. He asked no quarter and he gave none.

In the Preface to *Original Sin*, Edwards expressed the hope 'that the extensiveness of the plan of the following treatise will excuse the length of it' (p. 103), and he asked the reader's indulgence since it seemed to him necessary to deal with 'almost *every* argument advanced by the main opposers' at the same time that he had to present the arguments in defence of the doctrine in question. It is manifestly impossible, in view of Edwards's intricate examination of a text with which few readers are now familiar, to discuss the whole treatise; instead attention will be drawn to the main points with special emphasis on Edwards's original contributions to the topic. These are, as we shall see, of the utmost importance.

Following his usual method, Edwards's first task is to show the evidence of original sin to be found by observation and experience, and in the testimonies of Scripture. According to Edwards, the most common meaning of 'original sin' as used by divines is the '*innate sinful depravity of the heart*'. In addition, however, the phrase has come to include the *imputation* of Adam's first sin to posterity which now stands under the divine judgement. Edwards holds that the two go together and that proving one establishes the other.

Edwards lays it down as a first premise that the way we come by the ideas of disposition and tendency is by observing what is constant and general in the events that surround us in the world of nature and human society. This evidence is enhanced when a great variety of circumstances are taken into account and, especially, when the same effect continues despite great opposition standing in the way. For him, of course, the prevalence of effects is an indication of a current 'propensity' in mankind. He does not, however, want to claim that his opponents reject his first premise, but they do deny that corruption and moral evil prevail.

Actually, Taylor and others were not opposed to the idea of discovering general tendencies in experiences; on the contrary, they welcomed the idea but insisted that the true trend is to be found in the preponderance of goodness and virtue. Opponents of original sin claimed that Edwards was generalizing from the wrong sort of experience; thus George Turnbull (1698–1748) says 'As if a court of justice were a proper place to make an estimate of the morals of mankind, or an hospital of the healthfulness of the climate' (p. 108). Edwards finds the same view expressed by Taylor: 'We must not take measure of our health and enjoyments from a lazar-house, nor of our understanding from Bedlam, nor of our morals from a gaol' (ibid.). Those who argue in this way, says Edwards, are overlooking something essential, and which they too admit, namely, that we are to consider the innate disposition of man's heart *without* the *interposition of divine grace*, which is to say that man's evil tendencies would have had the most pernicious consequences 'were it not that the free mercy and kindness of God interposes to prevent that issue' (p. 109). Edwards's point here is two-fold; first, we are to consider the innate tendency of man *apart* from the divine intervention that actually took place, and, secondly, that no such intervention by God as is admitted on all sides would have been necessary were it not for man's innate evil disposition.

Edwards introduces a small arsenal of biblical passages to show that everyone comes into the world under the 'universal commission of sin' and that all sin deserves utter and eternal destruction. A few typical passages will suffice on both counts. 'If any man sinneth against thee, for there is no man that sinneth not' (1 Kings 8:46); 'There is not a just man upon earth, that doth good, and sinneth not' (Eccles 7:20); 'If we say that we have no sin, we deceive ourselves, and the truth is not in us'

(1 John 1:8); 'For as many as are of the works of the law are under the curse . . .' (Gal 3:10); 'By the works of the law shall no flesh be justified . . .' and all that seek to be justified by the works of the law 'are found sinners' (Gal 2:16, 17). Edwards concludes: 'here we are plainly taught, both that every one of mankind is a sinner, and that every sinner is under the curse of God' (p. 115).

It is important to take note here of another of Edwards's argumentative devices. The foregoing account of man's sinfulness and consequent guilt is part of a running commentary on Taylor's work on original sin. Leaving aside Edwards's criticism of that position, he is nevertheless at pains to show that Taylor agrees with him on the essential points. Edwards cites passage after passage from Taylor's text and then concludes:

> Now the reader is left to judge whether it ben't most plainly and fully agreeable to Dr. Taylor's own doctrine, that there never was any one person from the beginning of the world, who came to act in the world as a moral agent . . . but what is a sinner or transgressor of the law of God; and that therefore this proves to be the issue and event of things . . . that, by the natural and proper demerit of their own sinfulness . . . are the proper subjects of the curse of God. (p. 115)

Edwards now has Taylor on his own ground, so to speak, so that whatever differences between them may arise, both are arguing about the same doctrines—that man has an innate tendency to corruption and that all are under the condemnation of God.

One of Edwards's original contributions to the discussion is found in his attempt to deal with the basic idea of a natural tendency or propensity in the human constitution. This is a matter to be considered, he says, before it is determined whether this is a tendency to good or to evil. The point at which he was ultimately driving is rooted in his perception that there is far more evil in the world than can be accounted for by considering particular sinful acts one at a time. It is for this reason that he focused attention on the idea of tendency itself as the way of speaking about *sin* as a prevalent condition in contrast to *sins* as particular occasions of misdoing. As he put it, 'A notion of a stated tendency or fixed propensity is not obtained by observing only a single event' (p. 121). What is needed instead is a survey of many occasions in order to determine when a steady and common effect is manifest as following from the same causes and conditions.

It is through such observation that we discover the tendencies that exist in nature; it is ridiculous, says Edwards, for anyone to observe how regularly water quenches fire and then to claim that 'there was no tendency in it to such an effect'. The same holds true for human nature; it exists in an enormous variety of persons, places and circumstances, but throughout all this variety there *persists* the *tendency* to sinfulness as the common factor. Tendency, moreover, is not confined to individuals but extends to natural kinds, families and nations. In all these cases, Edwards says, we derive the notion of tendency—'a stated preponderation in causes'—by observing the prevalence of a particular kind of effect.

Edwards insists that the tendency in question does not consist in particular external circumstances, but is '*inherent*, and is seated in that *nature* which is common to all mankind, which they carry with them wherever they go . . .' (p. 124). The emphasis must fall upon man, and Edwards rejects the view that, while there may be this universal tendency in man, it does not lie in man's nature, 'but in the general constitution and frame of this world' (p. 125). Edwards's response to this 'evasion' is that if any creature prove itself evil in the proper place that God has assigned to it in the universe, it is of an evil nature. A stone, says Edwards in an illustration reminiscent of his earlier study of Newton's thought, is heavy by nature, but we might conceive of its being placed at a distance from this world where it would not have such a quality. We are, however, considering the world that God has made and hence the propensities of things are to be understood in terms of how they manifest themselves in their proper places. If, therefore, mankind has a universal tendency to sin in the place where God has placed it, this tendency must be regarded as belonging to human nature.

As we noted earlier, Edwards is arguing against what has come to be called the 'particularism' of the tradition of British empiricism expressed in the doctrine that all that 'really' exists is the individual case. This doctrine runs counter to any belief in natural kinds, tendencies or universal structures in the scheme of things and it received a classic formulation in *A System of Logic* (1843) by John Stuart Mill where he claimed that all reasoning is from particular to particular without the need for rational structures in between. Edwards found this conception of being too limited and insisted on the need to recognize the reality of the tendencies and propensities—what Charles Peirce would later call the *general*—that become manifest through a multitude of events and human actions. In this respect, Edwards, for all the emphasis that has been placed on his 'Idealism', was a realist in the philosophical sense; reality is not exhausted by particulars, because there are, as well, continuing structures in the natures of things which are real factors in determining how they will behave.

Having established his point about sin as the innate tendency to wickedness, Edwards proceeds to give an account of 'the many other things, that manifest a very corrupt tendency or disposition in man's nature in his present state' (p. 133). This account is long and complex in virtue of the fact that it is interspersed with Edwards's arguments against Taylor, Turnbull and others. A brief summary of the 'other things' Edwards has in mind must suffice.

Human depravity, he says, manifests itself not only in the universal tendency to sin, but in '*immediately* transgressing God's law' as soon as we have begun to act as moral agents. Depravity appears again in there being a much greater degree of sin than righteousness, both in substance and quantity. The law of God is love to God, but the tendency in all men is to withhold more of that love than they give, with the result that all have more sin than righteousness. Another evidence of wickedness is the folly and stupidity with which the things of religion are treated. Edwards cites two principal evils; proneness to idolatry, and disregard of eternal things. He calls idolatry folly because the one true God has been plainly revealed and only through human foolishness does anyone fall down before the sun, the moon, planetary deities, beasts and other idols. Nor did this happen only in ignorant and untaught countries, but in Greece, Egypt and Rome, the legendary habitations of learning. As regards the neglect of concern for our own good and destiny, Edwards quotes with approval an entire page from Locke's *Essay* in which he maintains that it is a failure of understanding on the part of those who cannot see that the infinite happiness of another life greatly outweighs riches, honour and worldly pleasure in this one. Edwards's comment is that it is evidence of a depraved disposition to act contrary to reason.

The next sign of human corruption is found in the fact that the greater part of mankind in every age have been wicked. To support this claim, Edwards says, we do not need to set ourselves up as judges of the heart; we have the words of Christ that strait is the gate and 'few there be that find it'. The reason that the precepts of the Beatitudes are difficult to follow is that they run counter to our natural inclinations and these stem from an innate corruption of the heart. Finally, human depravity explains why all great efforts to promote virtue in the world have had so few results.

Here Edwards is chiefly concerned with the record of God's activity on man's behalf—the sending of Noah as a warning, the deliverance from Egypt, the return from the Babylonian captivity, the raising up of Cyrus to punish Babylon, the raising up of prophets and of the great King David—all of which proved to be of little avail against the tide of human wickedness. Edwards asks his readers to consider 'the dreadful corruption of the present day' despite all the advantages of learning and philosophical knowledge which were achieved in the seventeenth and eighteenth centuries. In addition, there is a further inducement to virtue which this age enjoys; man's life has been shortened to seventy or eighty years as compared with a 'near thousand' and thus the time in which to commit evil deeds has been greatly diminished! One can only speculate about whether Edwards would have viewed the increase in longevity of recent decades as but further evidence of man's depravity.

One of the most interesting parts of *Original Sin* is Edwards's treatment of what he calls 'several evasions' of his argument in support of human depravity. Once again, these cannot be considered here in great detail, but we can take account of the basic points and, in doing so, note the similarities between the explanations proposed and the various attempts made in our own time, especially on the part of social scientists, to absolve us from responsibility for much of the evil that is in the world.

The first evasion—Edwards cites five—is that Adam's nature was not sinful, yet he sinned and hence the doctrine of original sin is not needed to account either for the sin that is in the world or Adam's sin. Edwards's rejoinder is that it is a mistake to suppose that because an effect's being general does not alter the nature of the effect (as Taylor maintained), it makes no difference whether the cause operate in a steady manner or only once. For Edwards, failure to take the difference in the cause seriously is contrary to reason. That every effect has a cause, does not imply that a *transient* effect (Adam's initial disobedience) must have a *permanent* cause: 'one act don't prove a fixed inclination' (p. 191). If a tree produces fruit that is spoiled at a particular time, we cannot conclude that the nature of the tree is bad. That we could do only if that kind of tree in all soils, countries, seasons and climates uniformly produced bad fruit. So it is with human beings; we can argue to fixed principles and inclinations in people only from repeated and continued actions of a voluntary choice.

Edwards's point here is that the first sin of Adam without a previous disposition to sin has no force against his argument in support of a fixed propensity to sin in mankind. Regardless of the *extent* of Adam's sin and that of the angels, the *permanence* of the effect is something very different because it shows a fixed propensity; first acts taken by themselves, says Edwards, were *not* permanent effects.

The second evasion takes the form of the claim that regardless of the great and general extent of wickedness in the world, free will is sufficient to explain the consequences and there is no need to invoke human depravity. Here Edwards repeats much of what he has said many times before about the incoherence of the notion of the 'freedom of the will'—by which he meant contingency and freedom 'from' the constraint of previous inclination—but he adds a novel element. In view of the vast amount of evil in the world, Edwards asks, how does it happen that mankind so universally 'agree in this evil exercise of their free will?' (p. 194). If, Edwards contends, there is no natural tendency involved, there is as good a chance that good would predominate rather than evil. But, in his view, that does not actually happen because all history shows the opposite; millions in successive generations 'without consultation, all agree to exercise their freedom in favor of evil'.[7]

The third evasion consists in the claim that the corruption in the world is not the result of human depravity, but is due to bad example and faulty instruction.[8] Edwards cites a passage from Taylor intended to illustrate the point; 'The Gentiles in their heathen state, when incorporated into the body of the Gentile world, were without strength, unable to help or recover themselves' (p. 196). Taylor's argument is that if there is no depravity of nature, what else could account for their plight but bad instruction and bad examples? Taking this claim at face value, Edwards has little difficulty showing that it moves around in a circle: ''Tis accounting for the thing by the thing itself. It is accounting for the corruption of the world by the corruption of the world' (p. 196). That bad examples are widespread or general Edwards takes to be a *description* of what has to be accounted for and hence it cannot be an explanation of man's situation. In short, these bad examples themselves can be accounted for only in terms of the general tendency to wickedness. To reinforce his point, Edwards goes on to cite some good examples and to ask why they had so little effect in turning the tide in the opposite direction. The first of these illustrations shows Edwards's ingenuity in handling Scripture. Acknowledging that the Bible gives only a brief account of the behaviour of Adam and Eve—'our first parents'—Edwards 'supposes' that 'before ever they had any children, they repented, and were pardoned, and became truly pious' (p. 196), so that God planted a noble vine at the beginning of mankind and pointed the 'stream of example' in the right direction.

The chief example of virtue is, of course, Jesus Christ—the example of examples—and were it not for human depravity, his example would have had greater influence among those who profess to be his followers than has become evident. The implication is clear, even if Edwards was fond of making his impact by leaving it implicit: if the giving of examples is one of God's wisest ways of leading his people, and if his best example did not, because of man's corruption, overcome the power of all the evil examples, how much less is it possible for bad example and instruction to be the cause of that corruption. Edwards is, as always, very perceptive: if the best does not succeed, how can the worst do better?

The fourth evasion is represented by an idea that has been proposed ever and again in discussions about human nature, namely, that in human development our senses mature first and our passions thus gain an advantage over our reason. The idea has its roots in the tendency of much ancient Greek philosophy to associate the appetite and the senses with evil and error and to think of reason as both the source of good and the power that is to guide and constrain sense and appetite.[9] Edwards does not deal with the problem here by attacking the dualism involved; instead, he allows it to stand and claims that what Taylor and Turnbull are proposing must face the same difficulties which they urge against God's so arranging things that men are brought into being with a propensity to sin. That is to say, if the strength of the sensitive appetites and habitual animal passions that are supposed to arise before the exercise of rational powers are to *account for* the wickedness in the world, they can do so only if they already imply a tendency to sin. Deeply rooted habits cannot explain what they are supposed to explain; they 'can't account for an effect which is supposed to have no tendency to that effect' (p. 202). In Edwards's judgement, we are brought back again to the doctrine of natural depravity via a detour through animal passions.

The fifth, and last, evasion is the claim that men are on trial in the world and that it is appropriate for them to have obstacles and temptations to overcome so that through conflict 'our virtue may be refined and established'. Edwards meets this challenge by invoking the conception of cause and effect with which we are by now familiar, and by posing the issue in the form of a dilemma. Either the temptations supposed to try men's souls amount to a prevailing tendency to the state of general wickedness which is admitted by all parties to be the case, or it does not. If we take the latter alternative that no prevailing tendency exists, says Edwards, there is no tendency to the effect in question. If, taking the other alternative, we say that the state of temptation does imply a prevailing tendency to the wickedness that is the ruin of mankind, 'it is a very evil, corrupt and dreadful state of things' (p. 205). Once again, we are back to an original corruption.

The general shape of the argument here is the same as we saw in the *Freedom of the Will*. Every attempt to provide an alternative to determinism leads either to incoherence—the infinite series of willing to will—or to determinism restored. So it is in *Original Sin*; every proposed substitute for human depravity as the cause of mankind's ruinous condition either fails to account for that condition—no real cause can be without a prevailing tendency—or it reinstates, by implication, the depravity insisted upon by the doctrine of original sin.

Having done this much in the way of discrediting the arguments of his opponents, Edwards has two more items on his agenda. He must deal with the thorny question—unavoidable by any form of theological determinism—as to whether God is to be seen as the author of sin. He must also consider the no less difficult problem of how we are to understand the imputation of Adam's sin to his offspring. Both of these matters have been on the periphery of the discussions we have followed thus far—God as the sole cause must in some sense be responsible for everything that happens; what is to be said of Adam's sin without there being a previous tendency—but in the latter part of the work Edwards devotes special attention to them. As will become evident, his treatment of the problem of imputation contains one of his most original ideas.

Edwards opens his discussion of the question: If God is the author of our being is he not also the author of our depravity?, by pointing out that Taylor includes within the conception of original sin a supposition that does *not* belong to it. This supposition is that nature must be corrupted by some *positive influence* or an *infection* altering its course. On the contrary, says Edwards, 'there is not the least need of supposing any evil quality *infused*, *implanted* or *wrought* into the nature of man, by any positive cause—either from God, or the creature' (pp. 380–1).

Man was made with two kinds of principles implanted in him; the first, called inferior or natural, are the principles of human nature—self-love, natural appetites and passions—the second, called superior and divine, comprise the divine love which is the image of God and man's righteousness. The first corresponds to what the Bible calls *flesh*, and the second to *spirit*. According to Edwards, these superior principles were meant to dominate the heart, while the lower were to be subservient. When man sinned and broke the covenant, the superior principles left his heart and the 'Holy Spirit, that divine inhabitant, forsook the house' (p. 382). Consequently, the inferior principles took command and, in Edwards's language, 'Man did immediately set up himself, and the objects of his private affections and appetites, as supreme; and so they took the place of God' (ibid.).

Man's eating the forbidden fruit, while but one act of sin, led to God's withdrawal from the rebellious self thus leaving the natural principles to themselves. There is no implanting of a bad principle by God such as would supposedly make him the author of depravity; man's wickedness and God's subsequent withdrawal are, says Edwards, 'sufficient to account for his becoming entirely corrupt'. The same is said to hold true of Adam's posterity. As God withheld his communion and grace from the 'common head' of mankind, so he does the same with all of Adam's successors. The central idea is, of course, God's 'withdrawal', for in this way Edwards can claim that, while God 'permits' sin, he is not the 'author' of it.[10] God, by withholding his grace, gives men up to their own lusts and affections and thus to the *continuance* of sin.

As a final thrust against Taylor, Edwards claims that if the permission of sin is the same as God's being the author of sin, 'then some things which Dr. Taylor himself lays down, will equally be attended with this very consequence' (p 384), since Taylor insists that God gives men up to their own wickedness. The implication is that unless Taylor accepts Edwards's distinction between permission and authorship of sin, he will be claiming that God is its author. In short, as Edwards said in other places, the Calvinists are in no better position than the Arminians on this crucial issue.[11]

Adam's posterity are born without holiness by the established course of nature, and by their continuing in corruption as individuals. Adam's posterity, according to Edwards, are from him, in him and belonging to him in an established order, just as the branches are related to the tree. The natural order has no independence of God, but is the order through which God immediately works his will. Edwards, however, wants to make it clear that the depravity of posterity is not due to the course of nature alone; there is, as well, the just judgement of God in the punishment of sin. Edwards closes this part of the discussion by insisting again on the parallel between Adam and his posterity. Adam continued in a state of unrighteousness after he had lost his righteousness through disobedience according to God's established order. 'I think', says Edwards, 'it is as truly, and in the same manner, owing to the course of nature, that Adam's posterity come into the world without original righteousness, and that Adam continued without it, after he had once lost it' (p. 386). In the end, Edwards sees the fault wholly in Adam's disobedience; God is not the author of sin. Edwards is, however, concerned that this matter not be confused with the closely related issue that has to do with the supposed injustice of charging Adam's sin to his successors. To that issue Edwards devotes his next chapter in the concluding Part of the work.

In view of the degree of sophistication evident in Edwards's thought, especially in comparison with many of his contemporaries, it is not easy to resist the temptation to exaggerate the cogency of his many arguments. As we have seen, Edwards had his own devices for dealing with opponents; he could avail himself of common sense and the 'vulgar' meanings of terms when that suited his purpose, or he could urge the superiority of a philosophical meaning of a term against the ordinary meaning. When he found himself in a logical bind, he could claim that in any case the views of his opponents are subject to the same difficulties and hence they are no better off.

When we come, however, to his discussion of the imputation of Adam's sin to his posterity, no one can reasonably deny the philosophical originality and the brilliance with which he handles the problem. With the possible exception of the concept of religious affections which was entirely original with Edwards, his analysis of the relation of Adam to his progeny and the consequent justification of imputing to mankind Adam's sin surpasses in insight and cogency anything he had ever written. For, while the doctrine of continuous creation to which he appealed was not new, his application of it in the context was novel, and in defending the reality of *kinds* (among which is mankind) against nominalism, he was entirely on his own. It was not until the writings of Charles Peirce over a century later that there appeared a more thorough account of the realistic position Edwards was arguing for.

In approaching the question of the imputation of Adam's sin, Edwards set two tasks for himself; first, to offer a correct *statement* of the doctrine, and, secondly, to show its reasonableness 'in opposition to the great clamor raised against it'. Edwards states the central point at the outset: God, in each step of his dealings with Adam within the framework of the covenant, 'looked on his posterity as being one with him' (p. 389). And, although God dealt 'more immediately' with Adam, he did so as the root of the whole tree and also with all the branches 'as if they had been existing in their root'. In dealing with the whole tree, says Edwards, God is also dealing with each *individual* branch and this is what is meant by the oneness or *identity* of Adam and his posterity. This is the contention that Edwards will expound and defend.

To begin with, says Edwards, it is a mistake to think of children coming into the world under a *double* guilt, the guilt of Adam's sin *and* the guilt of their own corruption; for there is only one guilt—'the guilt of the original apostasy, the guilt of the sin by which the *species* first rebelled against God' (p. 390, italics added). We are guilty for our own corruption continuing, but the guilt arising from our own depravity is not distinct from the guilt incurred by Adam.

Edwards explains the point by noting a two-fold disposition in Adam; there is, first, the evil inclination in Adam's heart that led to the first act of sin, and, secondly, there is the evil disposition as a confirmed principle that came as the result of God's forsaking him. The same is said to hold for Adam's posterity. Our corrupt dispositions are not to be regarded as belonging to us, but to our participation in Adam's sin, what Edwards calls the 'extended pollution of that sin'. Depravity as an established principle in us is a punishment of the first apostasy and brings new guilt.

Noteworthy in this account is Edwards's idea that the evil disposition in all is not a *consequence* of the imputation of Adam's sin, but rather *antecedent* to it since, to continue Edwards's figure, his rebellion *coexists* in the root and branches as a consequence 'of the union, that the wise Author of the world has established between Adam and his posterity' (p. 391). Both depravity and imputation stem from this union, but the evil disposition comes first and the charge of guilt follows.

Ever concerned about the proper understanding of God's role in dealing with Adam, Edwards appeals again to God's *permission*. God is no more the author of the evil disposition in the child than he was in the father. God, to be sure, could have prevented this evil, but he withheld his spiritual influence and did not do so. Here Edwards speculates no further and ends with the comment that 'whatever mystery may be supposed in the affair, . . . no Christian will presume to say, it was not in perfect consistence with God's holiness and righteousness', and this despite Adam's not having been guilty of any offence before. It is clear that Edwards does not want to involve himself further in whatever 'mystery' there may be, because he is intent on pursuing his main point which is the *oneness* of the root and the branches. The consequence of this identity is that 'an evil disposition exists in the hearts of Adam's posterity, equivalent to that which was exerted in his own heart, when he ate the forbidden fruit' (p. 394). As the sequel makes clear, in arguing that God treats Adam and his posterity as *one*, Edwards was attacking the idea that God treats individuals *one at a time* instead of dealing with *mankind as a whole*.

Edwards's second task is to defend the reasonableness of his interpretation against Dr Taylor's 'vehement exclamations against [its] reasonableness and justice' (ibid.). Typically, Edwards reduces all the objections to one and makes that the target of his attack, and defence: 'All may be summed up in this, that Adam and his posterity are *not one*, but entirely *distinct agents*'. In direct response to this claim, Edwards appeals to the 'most evident and acknowledged fact' that God deals with Adam and his posterity as one, and 'that every individual of mankind comes into the world in such circumstances as that there is no hope or possibility of any other than their violating God's holy law . . .'. Edwards is content with this seemingly dogmatic statement at the outset because he clearly wants to get on with the chief arguments for establishing his position by refuting two objections that were made against the idea of the oneness of Adam and his posterity. First, he says, is the objection that such a relationship is *injurious* to Adam's posterity, and, second, there is the charge of *falsehood* involved in treating as one what are not one, but are entirely distinct. Edwards sets out to deal with both objections, but it is the second one that troubled him most because it touched one of the basic principles of his metaphysics.

As regards the objection that having Adam stand as the head of his progeny is injurious and hurtful to them, Edwards insists that the situation is just the opposite. We are, he says, better off that Adam stood for us than would be the case if everyone had to stand for him or herself individually. Here Edwards cites three reasons for his claim: Adam was as likely because of his 'natural talents' to persevere in obedience as each individual standing alone, and if we are one with him we might have had the benefit of his obedience as we now share his fall; with Adam as head there was a greater possibility of a happy outcome because he had a stronger motive to be cautious than any of his successors since he had to stand for them as well as for himself; Adam was in a state of *complete manhood* at his trial, whereas all his followers only gradually mature and become moral agents so that each individual would be less able to stand for themselves than Adam was.

Having met the first objection, Edwards goes on to the more serious matter of defending his view against the charge that it runs counter to the true nature of things in treating as one what is not one, but wholly distinct. This charge, he says, is based on a false notion of what is meant by sameness or oneness among created things. Following his usual pattern, Edwards first states his thesis concisely and then develops it in detail. That thesis is that 'created identity or oneness with past existence, in general, depends on the sovereign constitution and the law of the Supreme Author and Disposer of the universe' (p. 397). Some things, Edwards says, are entirely distinct, but 'are so united by the established law of the Creator . . . that . . . it is with them as if they were one' (ibid.).

Edwards, as we can see, had not studied Newton in vain. The great tree a century old is distinct from the little sprout from which it came and with which it has been in constant succession, and while not one atom remains the same, 'yet God, according to an established law of nature, has in a constant succession communicated to it many of the same qualities . . . as if it were one' (pp. 397–8). The same is true of the mature individual whose body is one with the infant body from which he or she developed and, although 'the greater part of the substance probably changed scores (if not hundreds) of times',[12] God, 'according to the course of nature, which he has been pleased to establish', has caused a 'communication' between the infantile and the mature body and he thus treats the individual as *one* body. The same is said to hold true of mind and body; taken individually, they are very different but by divine constitution they are strongly united and become one.

Edwards now turns to the basis for personal identity in intelligent beings and, as was noted previously in the discussion of Edwards's relation to Locke's thought, he says that while Locke's appeal to the *same consciousness* points to an essential element, it is not all that is involved. The continuation of the same consciousness, says Edwards, is itself dependent on a law of nature established by God. Here again, Edwards is arguing against the belief held by many Deists that the course of nature, once established, goes on to work of itself. Edwards is pleased to point out that Taylor agrees with his contention that the course of nature separate from God 'is no cause, or nothing'. Edwards also notes that his other opponent, Dr Turnbull, cites Newton's view that the mind is the first cause of all laws of nature. Personal identity depends everywhere and always on God's sovereign constitution, as indeed does every created being. Nothing presently existing, says Edwards, is the result of its past existence alone because that past existence itself depends on God's original creation. To remain in existence, moreover, all beings require God's *continuous* creation without which they would lapse into nothing.

This excursion into metaphysics is essential to Edwards's argument for the unity of mankind and its relation to Adam. If the existence of created substance is the effect of God's continuously creative power, what exists at any moment is not dependent on its past existence but is a *new effect*. I, at present, am not the same as my past existence, but the Creator so unites these successive new effects that '*he treats them as one*, by communicating to them like properties, relations and circumstances' (p. 403). Thus my continuing identity as one person is the result of God's continuous creation.

According to Edwards, what takes place with respect to each individual also takes place with respect to all individuals considered as a species. The posterity of Adam must be regarded as *one* with him:

> I am persuaded no solid reason can be given, why God, who constitutes all other created union or oneness according to his pleasure, . . . may not establish a constitution whereby the natural posterity of Adam . . . should be treated as one with him, for the derivation, either of righteousness and communion in rewards, or in the loss of righteousness and consequent corruption and guilt.

In support of his contention, Edwards cites the arrangement of the natural world in which there is an 'apparent manifold analogy through the whole system of nature in this lower world' (p. 406). Accordingly, all parts of the world 'are derived from the *first of the kind*, as from their root and fountain'. Individuals derive from this root all the properties and qualities proper to the nature of the kind or species to which they belong. The central point is that Edwards is calling attention to God's having constituted *mankind*—'all are made of one blood, to dwell on all the face of the earth'— whereby all are united in society to partake together in the natural and common goods and evils of human life in the world. Here Edwards is attacking the idea that, as Taylor argued, sorrow and shame can only be for *personal* sin and that we can repent only of that sin with no regard for the sins of others. 'Nor is it a strange thing and unheard of', says Edwards, 'that men should be ashamed of things done by others, whom they are nearly concerned in' (p. 407). The corruption of mankind, in short, cannot be accounted for by considering the sins of each individual taken one at a time.

Edwards concludes that there is no reason standing against his contention that the race of mankind 'partake of the sin of the first apostasy'; it becomes *their* sin because of the real union that exists between the root—Adam—and the human race. In a bold stroke, Edwards declares that the sin of Adam's posterity is not the *result* of God's imputing that sin to mankind; on the contrary, the consent of his posterity to the first apostasy makes the sin properly *theirs*, and it is upon that ground that God imputes it to them.

It seems clear that what troubled Edwards most in the entire controversy about the doctrine of original sin was the repeated charge that it proved God to be unjust. In response, Edwards insisted that in consideration of the fact that the course of things in the universe is dependent on the sovereign constitution 'of the supreme Author' whose ways 'are past finding out', common modesty should be sufficient to lead people to refrain from making judgements about the justice of God. For the derivation of depravity and guilt from Adam to his posterity is 'taught in his Holy Word', to which Edwards as philosopher adds: 'a thing so abundantly confirmed by what is found in the experience of all mankind in all ages'.

Notes

1 Since Edwards's original title was even longer than the above, I shall use the short title, *Original Sin*, as adopted by *The Works of Jonathan Edwards* 3 (New Haven and London: Yale University Press, 1970). The work was edited by the late Clyde A. Holbrook. The reader is urged to consult the editor's Introduction for valuable information about the work and especially Edwards's sources—John Taylor, George Turnbull, Francis Hutcheson, John Locke and others. Page references in the text are to this edition.

2 It is interesting to note that, among all the great representatives of the Enlightenment in England, France and Germany, only one, Immanuel Kant, took the Reformation emphasis seriously. We see this in the section 'Radical evil in human nature' in *Religion Within the Limits of Reason Alone* (1793).

3 Edwards was clearly uneasy about imputing motives, at least to some of his opponents, in the matter of their using artful methods to deceive readers—the most obvious being to claim to venerate Paul and then proceed to offer 'new' interpretation of his writings. Hence he says that many of these interpreters were probably sincere in believing that they were faithfully representing Paul's doctrines—whether they *intended* to deceive readers or not, their practices in interpretation nevertheless have that effect.

4 There is, of course, abundant evidence of Edwards's ability in scriptural interpretation and in every dimension—linguistic, grammatical and semantic. His *Miscellanies*, *Sermons*, the so-called 'Blank Bible'—a Bible with interleaved blank pages on which to make exegetical commentary—and a body of as yet unpublished writings on the Bible, testify to his awesome command of the material. See *Apocalyptic Writings*, ed. Stephen J. Stein, *The Works of Jonathan Edwards* 5 (New Haven and London: Yale University Press, 1977).

5 *Original Sin*, ch. IV, section 1, pp. 306ff.

6 For the sake of argument, nothing in what is cited from Taylor prevents him from being 'certain' that death in the temporal sense persists in the verses in question, but without having to claim that it is the *only* meaning present.

7 Edwards has not been credited with having a great sense of humour, but that he was not without it appears here very nicely in the phrase 'without consultation'. Millions express their freedom in the same way without the need to discuss the matter with each other!

8 A variation on this theme found expression in the earlier decades of this century through the idea of the 'cultural lag'. The problems confronting society, including the misuse of human freedom, would be much more open to solution when the sciences of man finally caught up with the great achievements of the natural sciences in the control of nature. A favourite anecdote of the late Reinhold Niebuhr was about a small boy who slapped his sister for no apparent reason; the nurse attending to both said 'I wonder what bad boys taught him to do a thing like that?'

9 Augustine overcame this dualism through the Christian conception of the natural man of 'flesh' who is a *unity* of body, mind and spirit. Sin cannot be attributed exclusively to the body and the senses because it infects the person as a whole including mind or reason. In his discussion of *concupiscence*, Augustine insisted that inordinate desire is not to be put down to the senses and the body alone since reason is involved as well in the form of an idea that indicates the nature of what is desired. In short, only a *rational* being is capable of concupiscence. Many treatments of this topic have suffered from the confusion of 'flesh' with 'body' so that the war between the 'man of flesh' and the 'spiritual man' is made into a conflict between mind and body. The man of flesh in the New Testament is the *whole* natural man and not some particular property or faculty, and it is this man who is at odds with the spiritual man.

10 Edwards bolsters his argument by referring to what he had written earlier in *Freedom of the Will*: *The Works of Jonathan Edwards* 1 (New Haven: Yale University Press, 1957), pp. 397ff., where he says much the same thing.

11 See Perry Miller, *Jonathan Edwards* (New York: William Sloane Associates, 1949), p. 259 where he quotes Edwards as saying in this connection, it is 'a difficulty wherein the Arminians share with us'.

12 Edwards anticipates the point that was later made by Whitehead under the aegis of the new physics and physiology; our bodily material recycles itself every seven years so that individual identity and unity cannot be accounted for through that material alone.

6

Edwards's theological ethics and moral philosophy

Edwards's views concerning the nature of divine love or charity and his conception of a virtuous or holy life are expressed in three principal works: *Charity and its Fruits* (hereafter, *Charity*) and *Two Dissertations* the first of which has the title *Concerning the End for which God Created the World* (hereafter, *End of Creation*), and the second is *On the Nature of True Virtue* (hereafter, *True Virtue*).[1] *Charity* consists of fifteen sermons that Edwards preached in 1738 on 1 Corinthians 13, St Paul's well-known discourse on Christian love. The work was first published by Tryon Edwards in 1852 with the title that it still bears. The *Dissertations*, as Ramsey points out, were meant to be published together since the 'end' for which God created the world must also be the 'end' of a virtuous life.[2]

The first sermon in *Charity* is entitled 'Love the Sum of All Virtue', and Edwards begins by saying that charity and Christian love are the same, but that in the New Testament 'charity' is used in a much wider sense than what is meant by the term in ordinary discourse. The ordinary meaning includes thinking the best of people, putting a 'good construction on their words or behavior', and sometimes the disposition to give to the poor. Edwards, however, regards these things as but a part or fruit of charity as a virtue. In its Christian meaning, charity signifies both love to men and love to God. Edwards focuses attention on St Paul's recounting of the excellent things that one may have—speaking with the tongues of men and angels, the gift of prophecy and all knowledge, the faith to move mountains, bestowing all goods on the poor, offering one's body as a sacrifice—and his claim that all of these come to *nothing* without *charity*; and he derives from Paul's words the doctrine—'All that virtue which is saving, and distinguishing of true

Christians from others, is summed up in Christian or divine love'.[3]

Edwards, as always, was an ontological thinker which is also to say a theological thinker; he ever and again sought to trace things back to principles. In developing the meaning of divine love, Edwards began with the meaning of self-love. Not unmindful of the command to love God with all one's being and the neighbour 'as thyself'—a measure that has been the subject of extended discussion over the centuries within Christianity—Edwards sets out to consider the nature of self-love. His first distinction is between a *selfishness* that is objectionable because it is confined to a narrow and exclusive love of self as if it were the entire universe, and a universal love of self that expresses our human capacity to love our own happiness which for Edwards is the same as having a will.

This distinction is so important for Edwards's conception of Christian virtue under the commandment to love God and neighbour that we must consider it at greater length. Edwards repeatedly insists that 'a Christian spirit is not contrary to all self-love' (p. 254) nor is Christianity opposed to a person's loving himself which he equates with loving his own happiness:

> Christianity is not destructive of humanity. That a man should love his own happiness is necessary to his nature, as a faculty of will is; and it is impossible that it should be destroyed in any other way than by destroying his being.[4]

Selfishness, however, is contrary to a Christian spirit and Edwards goes on to indicate what is meant by the 'inordinate' self-love which is for him identical with selfishness. When a person is redeemed, says Edwards, it is not by a reduction of his love to happiness, 'but only by regulating it with respect to its exercises and influence, and the objects to which it leads' (p. 255). Here Edwards is choosing his words very carefully; the root meaning of 'inordinate' is to be 'unregulated' or 'without measure'. Self-love becomes inordinate in two respects; first, it may be of so great a degree that it surpasses love to others and in this way comes to have undue influence on the person; secondly, self-love can be 'placed' in the wrong channel, as when the person sees his own happiness only 'in things that are confined to himself' so that others are excluded. This, Edwards writes, 'is the thing most directly intended by that self-love which the Scripture condemns' (p. 257). The Christian spirit, to the contrary, seeks not only its own things, but the things of others, and it also may require that we part with what we have for the good of others.

Edwards expresses the difference between the self-love that

degenerates into selfishness and the self-love as it exists under the principle of divine love in specifically theological terms: 'The ruin which the Fall brought upon the soul of man consists very much in that he lost his nobler and more extensive principles, and fell wholly under the government of self-love' (p. 252). Edwards sees the difference between the soul before the Fall and after in terms of expansion and contraction. When man was governed by divine love, his soul was 'enlarged to a kind of comprehension of all his fellow creatures' (p. 253) and was not limited by the bounds of the creation, but 'dispersed itself abroad in that infinite ocean of good'. After the transgression, 'those nobler principles were immediately lost and all this excellent enlargedness of his soul was gone and he thenceforward shrunk into a little point, circumscribed and closely shut up within itself to the exclusion of others' (ibid.).

Edwards makes it quite clear that the love of our own happiness is not to be construed solely in terms of the narrow and limited self, but must include all, i.e., mostly objects other than the self, that is 'grateful' or the character in something to which our appropriate response is *gratitude*.[5] It is this apprehension of all that goes to make up human happiness that takes us beyond the narrow and confined self.

Edwards was concerned to show that the Christian spirit does not run counter to a proper self-love, because as love of our happiness it is natural and hence there is nothing inherently wrong about it. He goes even further and says that having such love is the same as having a will, so that if self-love were set at naught we would have to deny the very characteristic that sets us apart from stones and stars. As Ramsey puts it, Edwards saw the universal love of our happiness as what 'makes the world go around' (p. 16).

Universal love, however, although essential, does not suffice since it must be combined with 'another principle' that involves, as Edwards says, 'uniting a person with another'. Edwards's idea is that universal self-love does not of itself inform us of *what* and *whom* we are to love; love to particulars requires recourse to another principle. What this principle implies is that love of what delights us must include the happiness of another. The commandment to love is two-fold—love of God and love of the neighbour, and Edwards is trying to show how the two are related as *particular* loves and joys that stem from a universal self-love 'compounded' by another principle. How, in short, do we come to see that love and praise to God is the happiness that self-love seeks and that the happiness of another person is included in our happiness?

According to Ramsey, Edwards answers these questions most clearly in a 'Miscellany' dealing with 'compounded self-love', where it is said to arise

> from the necessary nature of a perceiving and willing being, whereby he loves his own pleasure or delight; but not from this alone, but it supposes also another principle, that determines the exercise of this principle, and makes that to become its object which otherwise cannot: *a certain principle uniting this person with another*, that causes the good of another to be its good. The first arises simply from his own being whereby that which agrees immediately and directly with his own being is his good; the second arises also from *a principle uniting him to another being*, whereby the good of other being does in a sort become his own.[6]

Love of neighbour stems from the love of God that is common to us so that our self-love is now channelled in a *particular* direction that takes it far beyond the confines of a self-love that is exclusive.

It is important to understand that, for Edwards, knowledge of God in the understanding and love of God in the will or heart means our *participation in* God's knowledge of himself and our *partaking of* divine love. The ambiguity in 'knowledge of God'—that it can mean either our knowledge of God, or God's knowledge of himself—and the ambiguity in 'love of God' that it can mean either our love of God or God's own love—is overcome by Edwards through the idea that only *one* meaning is present. That is, if there is any knowledge of God and love of God in any created being, that can mean only that one participates in God's knowledge of himself or is infused by the divine love. The doctrine upon which Edwards bases this conclusion is that the *only* knowledge of God there is is God's knowledge of himself which is communicated to us through the Word, and all love to God in the creatures is from 'the love of God's being in them'.

The emphasis here on God as the only effective power in the world, the supreme cause that acknowledges no 'secondary' causes among the creatures—the belief that led William Ellery Channing (1780–1842) to place Edwards among the pantheists for whom the mystery is why there is anything else but God—has to be understood against the background of what we may call Edwards's grand strategy. According to that strategy, it is necessary to take seriously into account all that belongs to nature and to nature's God as part of God's total providential design, but at the same time to show that the natural falls short of grace. Accordingly, in his treatment of our moral nature, Edwards is concerned to recognize the validity of natural benevolence or concern for the good of others and not set it at nought and yet he is determined to show that it does not suffice. True virtue, the mark of 'saving' operations, goes beyond the most remarkable accomplishments of the natural man. Edwards's ultimate concern is to depict man as the 'new creation' in Christ of which Paul spoke so eloquently, the being who is filled with the knowledge and love of God and who, as the redeemed man, is the end sought by God in creation. In pursuit of his goal, Edwards discusses at length, focusing on the thought of the British moral philosopher Francis Hutcheson (1694–1746),[7] the rationalist's idea of disinterested benevolence as the criterion for moral judgement. To anticipate the outcome, we may say that Edwards saw this criterion as only a calculation of pleasure against pain—something that nature can achieve on its own account—whereas true virtue is different in kind because it has to do with another dimension or what Edwards called the 'consent of beings to Being'—the philosophical counterpart of 'love to God'. Here, in the spirit of Edwards, we might add 'disinterested benevolence' to Paul's list of gifts in 1 Corinthians 13—'though I have such benevolence to the highest degree and have not charity, I am nothing'.

The parallel between what Edwards was doing in finding distinguishing marks of truly gracious affections in the appraisal of heart religion and what he is doing here in the delineation of true virtue is clear. In both cases he aimed to set forth what goes beyond the capacity of nature and the natural man and thus to delineate the new dimension represented in the work of the Spirit as the power of grace. Gracious affections stand beyond the 'natural' affections of which all are capable, and true virtue, or divine love, stands beyond the disinterested benevolence that marks the ultimate achievement of the 'natural' man. It is important to notice, however, that in neither case was he concerned to discount entirely the 'natural' component.

In speaking of the duty of a Christian spirit to do good to others, Edwards sets forth three considerations to be taken into account; the act itself, to whom we should do good, and the manner in which we do it. The most excellent way, says Edwards, is to do good to the souls of others, by which he means instructing them in the things of religion, counselling and warning those who are lax and even reproving those who fail in their duty. Above all is the setting of a good example; words, says Edwards, without an example 'will not be very likely to take effect' (p. 207). In addition to this spiritual help, Edwards cites the giving of goods to those in need, taking pains to promote the welfare of another and the suffering that goes with the effort to lighten another's burden.

To whom should we seek to do good? Edwards answers that in Scripture the 'neighbor' is the proper object of our actions, and he goes on to point out that Jesus' parable of the Good Samaritan was his response to the lawyer who, 'willing to justify himself', asked 'And who is my neighbor?' Despite the enmity between Jews and Samaritans, the Samaritan came to the aid of the Jew who had fallen among thieves and thus treated him as a neighbour. For Edwards, this relationship is meant to be mutual, 'equally predicable of both' and from this fact he drew three corollaries—that we should do good to both *good* and *bad* (although we 'should more abound in beneficence . . . to them who are of the household of faith'); to both *friends* and *enemies*; and to the *thankful* and the *unthankful*—and all this because we would 'imitate our Father which is in Heaven'.

In what manner should we seek to do good? Edwards's answer, as he says, is expressed in one word—'freely'. That is to say, kindness is the disposition to do good freely, and again from this disposition, Edwards draws three corollaries. We are not to do good for mercenary reasons, as if we were hired to do so or expected a reward. We must do good cheerfully and not grudgingly and, finally, we must be open-hearted and open-handed, giving without stint.

'The main thing', Edwards writes, 'in that love, which is the sum of the Christian spirit, is benevolence or good will to others' (p. 212), and he calls that 'love of benevolence' or 'that disposition which a man has who desires or delights in the good of another'. In characteristic fashion, Edwards ends this portion of the sermon with an emphasis on *practice*: 'The proper evidence of wishing good to another is doing good to another' (p. 213). It is ultimately in the deed that we find the presence of love.

Edwards, as we can see from the amount of space he devoted to the topic, was greatly concerned to show that Christian love is contrary to a selfish spirit, and in doing so he gives further insight into the manner in which we are to regard the neighbour. Edwards begins by focusing on what we are to understand by 'loving our neighbor as ourselves'. This second part of the Great Commandment, says Edwards, is contrary to selfishness because it requires us to look beyond ourselves, 'to look on their neighbor as being, as it were, one with self, and not only to consider our own circumstances and necessities, but to consider the wants of our neighbors as we do our own . . . to make their case our own, and to do to them as we would that they should do to us' (p. 265). At this point Edwards enters into what he himself calls a 'digression'—from the main point which is to show that love to neighbour is contrary to selfishness—which throws a great deal of light on his conception of the continuity, but also the difference, between the Old Testament and the Gospel. The duty to love others is not new; the same kind of love was required by the commandment of Moses, but it remains to explain why Christ said 'A new commandment I give unto you'.

It is new because, says Edwards, the 'rule and motive' of the commandment is new; in the old view the rule and motive was love to ourselves and that we should love our neighbours as ourselves, but in the Gospel view the rule and motive is the love of Christ for us—'that ye love one another, as I have loved you' (John 15:12) (p. 266). Edwards makes the comparison quite explicit when he writes:

> That we should love one another as we love ourselves is Moses' commandment . . . that we should love one another as Christ love[d] us is Christ's commandment. (ibid.)

Edwards's 'digression' at this point is no mere intrusion into his argument, but rather the establishing of a new vantage point for spelling out the fuller meaning of love of neighbour and for consolidating his thesis that it runs counter to a selfish spirit. Edwards cites four ways in which Christ's love for us was expressed. Christ set his love on those who were enemies to him, which is to say that he loved those who had no love for him. Christ's love, moreover, was such that 'he was pleased in some respects to look upon us as himself . . . and united his heart to them' (p. 266). In the beginning of the passage, however, Edwards spoke of 'love to men' (p. 267) but in the sequel the referent changes—'His elect were from all eternity dear to him, as the apple of his eye'—and it was for them that Christ looked upon their concerns, interests and guilt as his own. In describing the third expression of Christ's love, Edwards returns to 'us' and says that he spent himself 'for us' in forgoing his own ease and comfort and his honour in offering himself as a sacrifice to the justice of God. From this Edwards concludes that Christ loved us without any expectation of our love in return, and he makes the application at once—'our love to others will not depend on their love to us; but we shall do as Christ did to us, love them, though enemies' (p. 267).

The reason Edwards took such pains to show that love is opposed to selfishness is found in his concern to make a proper place for the self-love that is *not* inordinate but belongs essentially to human nature. Here, as in so many of his writings, Edwards's negatives are of the utmost importance and serve to make clear the true nature of something through vivid contrasts. The point, however, goes even deeper than contrasts and showing what love or affections are *not*; it involves Edwards's great concern to distinguish between two ideas, attitudes, motives which are *similar* in some respects, but are *not* the *same*, in order to explain why people mistake one for the other. As we shall see, there is a most telling example of this concern in *True Virtue* (ch. VII), the title of which speaks for itself: 'The reasons why those things that have been mentioned, which have not the essence of true virtue, have yet by many been mistaken for true virtue'. Hence, Edwards's method, while it includes in this case showing what true virtue is *not*, also directs attention to what is *similar* in the negative case to true virtue, but is not identical with it, hence a source of confusion.[8]

We must, nevertheless, not lose sight, as indeed Edwards did not, of the positive and the true virtuous life, because his method of negatives was meant to make the genuine form of virtue stand out more clearly than it otherwise would. We see this very well when we consider the moral *progression* that Edwards envisages in the Christian life. As Ramsey has pointed out, there is a parallel between this progression ending with the 'concatenation' of the graces in the fullness of love, and the eschatological movement wherein that fulfilment is seen as the 'end for which God created the world'. Even in Edwards's earliest reflections about God, Being, the consent to Being, excellency and the divine *gloria*, there is to be found a recurrent theme; God wants out of the depths of his love to have in the creation a being capable of *appreciating* the beauty—'excellency' in one of its several meanings—and the splendour of the divine *gloria* as it appears in the creation. It is in this sense that Edwards understood God's end in creation as the full manifestation of his own glorious nature; what better way to achieve this end than through the person of true virtue whose life, imbued with grace and the divine Spirit, shines forth with the fullness of holy love and practice.

The title of the present chapter, 'Edwards's theological ethics and moral philosophy', is meant to indicate two strands in his thought—Ramsey calls them the 'two sources of morality'—concerning human nature and conduct. We may identify these two strands as common morality from natural principles and as specifically Christian morality based on holy love and benevolence to God. There is, in short, a morality of nature and a morality of grace, a distinction employed by Edwards throughout his many writings and in different contexts. In his appraisal of the Awakening, for example, he treated common grace in his treatise, *Some Thoughts*, and concluded that 'on the whole and in general' the Awakening was truly a work of the divine Spirit. In *Religious Affections*, on the other hand, he was concerned exclusively with the signs of *gracious* affections which serve to distinguish the life of the saints beyond anything that can be achieved by the natural man.[9]

Thus far we have been dealing with Edwards's conception of Christian morality rooted in charity and manifested in its fruits. We must now turn to his treatment of common morality and his pursuit of 'the essence of true virtue'. First, however, a word of caution about Edwards's procedure is in order if confusion is to be avoided.

In *Charity* and in the *End of Creation*, Edwards was dealing with pure benevolence and the biblical understanding of the nature of Christian love as distinct from, but still related to, common morality based on natural principles. In *True Virtue*, which is intended to develop the chief features of common morality and also to point out the reasons why people mistake one for the other, Edwards *begins with* another account of the pure benevolence that characterizes Christian morality and this may confuse the reader. The reason for this starting point, however, is quite clear; Edwards wants to set before us the conception of true virtue as a basis for comparison and for showing why common morality, even in its highest form, falls short of Christian charity.

In seeking to understand what Edwards meant by true virtue, we need to recall the importance he attached to beauty, harmony and 'fittingness' or excellence as marks of divinity.[10] Hence, Edwards begins the dissertation with these words:

> Whatever controversies and variety of opinion there are about the nature of virtue, yet all (excepting some skeptics who deny any real difference between virtue and vice) mean by it something *beautiful*, or rather some kind of *beauty* or excellency. (p. 539)

He goes on to say that not all beauty can be called virtue, but only that beauty belonging to beings having perception and will. This characterization, however, is still too broad, because there is a beauty in speculation and the ideas of great thinkers, but, says Edwards, this is different from what is 'commonly meant' by virtue. The distinguishing feature must be found in the beauty of those acts of the mind that are of a *moral* nature and have to do with praise and blame. These, in turn, refer to will and disposition which Edwards sums up in the term 'heart', so that when we ask for the meaning of true virtue we must seek to determine what makes any habit or exercise of the heart 'truly *beautiful*'.

Edwards next distinguishes between a particular and a general beauty; the former is when something appears beautiful only in relation to some things within a limited sphere, as when a few notes in a tune are harmonious within themselves, but may prove discordant when considered in relation to the tune as a whole. General beauty, on the contrary, is beautiful 'as it is in itself' and as it stands connected with everything it has to do with. Edwards is working toward the definition of true virtue in terms of what he described in many writings as 'the consent of beings to Being in general', or God. Using the term 'benevolence' in the sense of 'consent, propensity, and union of heart', Edwards can define true virtue as 'benevolence' to Being in general, something that is exercised in a general good will. He is willing to admit that a person can be disposed to have benevolence to some particular being or a number of beings and that such a tendency can be good in some respects, but since such benevolence is not to Being in general it is not of the nature of true virtue. Edwards is emphatic on the point; the central virtue of love must have as its direct and immediate object Being in general or, as he sometimes puts it, 'the great system of universal existence'. Consent to anything less is inadequate.

Edwards, moreover, is not content merely to assert his claim. He offers several quite subtle arguments aimed at showing that virtue cannot consist in any love to its object because of its beauty, nor can we say that virtue consists in love to virtue, for that would be going around in a circle. We would be supposing that virtue is *both* the cause and effect of virtue. Using a form of the infinite regress argument that he had so often invoked in the *Freedom of the Will*, Edwards claims that if virtue consists in love to virtue, then what is loved is the love of virtue, and virtue becomes the love of the love of virtue and so on without end. The central point can be simply stated: since, according to Edwards, we are in search of the 'first benevolence' or benevolence which 'has none prior to it', this cannot consist in love to any particular beings on the basis of their *virtue*, their *beauty* or their *gratitude*, because that love *presupposes* a benevolence *prior* to each of the three which is their cause. Edwards claims that 'there is room for no other conclusion than that the primary object of virtuous love is Being, simply considered; . . . true virtue primarily consists . . . in a propensity and union of heart to . . . Being in general' (p. 544). In short, love to Being in general is the ultimate ground of virtue; to suppose any other object to fill this role is to be involved in an infinite regress.

Yet, Edwards continues, we are not to suppose that there is no virtue in any love other than absolute benevolence, since we must consider the good of particular beings in the light of our love to Being. If the good of a particular being is not so consistent or if there is any being that is opposed to Being in general, our consent to Being as such will induce 'the virtuous heart' to forsake that being. Thus Edwards is led to introduce what he calls a 'secondary object' of virtuous benevolence. Pure benevolence in its first exercise is, as we have seen, consent to Being, but there is a secondary object of virtue which Edwards calls 'benevolent being', or the presence of virtuous benevolence in its object. Hence when we, under the influence of general benevolence, see another being possessing the 'like general benevolence', our hearts are drawn to that person. We attach our hearts to him or her in the knowledge that he or she has the same love to Being that we have.

Edwards's idea is that our love to the other goes beyond the fact that the other exists, since he or she, in having love to Being in general, has their own being extended. We, in turn, motivated by that same love, 'must of necessity have . . . the greater degree of benevolence to him, as it were out of gratitude to him for his love to general existence' (pp. 546–7). Our hearts are extended to the other and we come to regard his or her interest as our own. Edwards, as we have seen many times, can follow up a complex and involuted expression of a basic idea with a quite simple summary, which in this case is that when the heart is united to

Being in general it looks upon a benevolent propensity to Being, 'wherever he sees it', as the beauty and excellency of the being who has it. Stated even more directly, Edwards is moving from the love of God to love of the neighbour.

The importance Edwards attached to the idea that the secondary ground or virtuous love arises solely from pure benevolence to Being in general can be seen in his spelling out six further considerations concerning the secondary ground.[11] These points can be summarized briefly, since they are largely corollaries of his main thesis. First, anyone who has a love to Being in general must love that same temper in others. Second, true moral or spiritual beauty is the secondary ground of virtue, including both qualities and exercises of the mind and the overt actions proceeding from them. Third, virtuous principles and acts are themselves beautiful because they imply consent and union with Being in general. Fourth, spiritual beauty, as a secondary ground, is the ground of both benevolence and complacence, but the former is the *primary* ground of the latter.[12] Fifth, whoever sees benevolence in two beings will value it more than in one alone, because it is more favourable to Being in general to have two beings to favour it than only one. Sixth, and most characteristic of Edwards's emphasis on the understanding heart, no one can relish the beauty of general benevolence 'who has not that temper himself'. The appreciation of that beauty in another reveals the true disposition of the heart.

We may now consider in summary fashion what Edwards took to be the main ingredients of common morality—secondary beauty, self-love, conscience and kindly affections—as a prelude to his discussion of 'the reasons why those things that have been mentioned (i.e., the ingredients just noted) which have not the essence of Virtue, have yet by many been mistaken for true Virtue'.[13] Edwards begins by repeating what he has said about primary beauty as the consent, agreement and union of beings to Being in mental or spiritual existence. There is, however, a secondary or inferior beauty—'which is some image of this'—that is not confined to spiritual beings but is found in inanimate things: the mutual agreement of the sides of a square or a regular polygon, the agreement of the colours, figures and distances between spots on a chessboard, the beauty of the figures on a piece of brocade. In all these cases, says Edwards, there is mutual agreement in form, manner, quantity and visible end or design which we express in such terms as regularity, order, uniformity, symmetry, proportion and harmony. Such beauty is an image of the primary beauty and serves as an analogy for God's work in patterning inferior things in accordance with what is superior. In so doing, God presents this inferior beauty, especially to those of a truly virtuous temper, as a way of making them aware of the divine love and of enlivening their sense of spiritual beauty.

As always, Edwards is concerned to point out that it is not by 'any reflection' upon the resemblance of secondary beauty to primary beauty that such things appear beautiful, but rather that 'their sensation of pleasure, on a view of this secondary beauty, is immediately owing to the law God has established, or the instinct he has given' (p. 567). Having the sensation of pleasure is the result of the cosmic harmony that endows us with the capacity to respond in just that way.

Edwards sees other virtues stemming from secondary beauty, such as *order in society* where all have appointed places and everyone keeps to his place, *wisdom* in the unifying of thoughts, ideas and actions to one general purpose, *justice*, or the harmonious system in which those who do evil will suffer evil in proportion to the evil done.[14] In this connection, Edwards speaks approvingly of Wollaston's[15] idea that all virtue can be resolved into an agreement of inclinations, volitions and actions with *truth*. Edwards interprets this in terms of justice between two beings so that in our duties and virtues we are to express such affections and behave toward another in a way that 'hath a natural agreement and proportion to what is in them, and what we receive from them' (p. 570), and he claims that here there is the same conformity of affection and action to its ground 'as that which is between a true proposition and the thing spoken of in it'.

The point is an important one because it involves the idea that, in Wollaston's words, 'A true proposition can be denied, or things may be denied to be what they are, by *deeds*, as well as by express words or another proposition'.[16] Hence there is a truth concerning actions no less than the more familiar truth of ideas. Most of the duties incumbent on us', Edwards writes, 'will be found to partake of the nature of justice' (p. 569). In short, secondary beauty is a major source of the common morality that makes possible the order of civil society.

The second principle of common morality is self-love, which Edwards defines in *True Virtue* as a 'man's love of his own happiness', except that there is an ambiguity in 'his own' which requires clarification. A man's 'own happiness', says Edwards, may be taken in a universal sense to include all the happiness or pleasure a man envisages—in which case self-love coincides with the general capacity of loving and hating—or it may mean the pleasure a person takes in a proper, private and separate good. That a person has the general capacity to love or be pleased does not of itself provide the reason why that love comes to be placed in any object, whether it be the love of neighbour or the glory of God. Edwards rejects, however, the view that our loving particular persons stems not from our love to happiness in general, but from a love to love our own happiness, because this would make the effect the cause of that which it is in the effect. Put more concretely, our happiness in the happiness of the beloved is made the *cause* of love to that person, but the truth is the other way around. Our love to the person is the cause of our delighting or being happy in his happiness.

As regards self-love in the sense of private interest, Edwards distinguishes between the pleasures and pains we have in participation with others—'by our hearts being united to them in affection'—and those that are originally our own and determined by inclinations implanted in us. If, says Edwards, we take self-love in the latter sense, love to others may really be one of its effects according to the laws of nature. To love those who are on our side and promote our interest is the natural consequence of self-love, and no other principle is required to bring about this effect. Having made this claim, however, Edwards, ever aware of counter-claims, takes note of those who say that some further principle is involved, especially for calling forth gratitude and anger, namely, a *moral sense*.[17]

The thesis Edwards is arguing against is: 'that the reason we are affected with gratitude and anger towards men, rather than things without life, is moral sense' (p. 580), or a principle of benevolence to others and love to the public which is present by nature in all mankind. But, says Edwards, if this is so, why do we not have grateful affections for the good done by inanimate objects—the sun and rain bring forth fruits for our benefit—and affections of anger at the mildew and overflowing streams which destroy these fruits? Edwards, in short, sees no need for a moral sense, since he believes that gratitude and anger can be accounted for through self-love and what he had previously said about our apprehensions of secondary beauty in things pleasing to us or in things to which we are averse. 'There are', he concludes, 'no particular moral virtues whatever, but what . . . come to have some kind of approbation from self-love, without the influence of a truly virtuous principle.'

The third principle or disposition in natural morality is conscience which, like the other ingredients, is regarded by Edwards as arising from self-love. The root meaning of conscience, for Edwards, is a disposition to be uneasy in a consciousness of being *inconsistent* with ourselves. To do to another person what we should be angry with him for doing to us, is to disagree with ourselves and to 'contradict ourselves'. In order to connect conscience and self-love, Edwards proposes a sort of parallel with pure love to others. In pure benevolence to others there is, as Edwards has put it several times before, a *union* of heart with the other and an enlargement of mind to include the other as one with ourselves. Likewise, self-love implies an inclination to feel and act *as one* to ourselves, and when we are inconsistent and feel and act in opposition to ourselves, uneasiness is the result. Having made this parallel, however,

Edwards feels compelled to interject a sharp distinction between natural and divine principles. Approving or disapproving of actions according to their agreement of disagreement with ourselves 'is quite a different thing' from approving or disapproving of them because we consent to and are united with Being in general. The later is a divine principle and the former a natural one.

No doubt one reason for this interjection is Edwards's concern to provide a basis for a discussion to come that deals with certain similarities between common morality and true virtue which lead people to mistake one for the other. But there appears to be something else involved, namely, Edwards's interest in relating the two moralities to each other even when he regards them as quite distinct. The problem becomes particularly acute in the case of virtues such as pity, gratitude and justice that appear in both moralities under the same names. It is best, however, to postpone further discussion of this point until we consider Edwards's reasons why the two moralities may be confused, and continue instead with the further analysis of conscience.

Matters of conscience, thinks Edwards, always involve relations to other people, the most basic of which is the capacity to put ourselves in their places. According to his conception of experience and of ideas, this capacity requires imagination and projection. Since Edwards holds that we have no ideas of any of our states—passions, affections, inclinations—except what we ourselves are conscious of 'the only knowledge we have of the inner life of other selves is by ascribing to them "ideas" we have of ourselves'.[18] Nor is this requirement confined to the experience of human selves; Edwards goes on to say that we could have no idea of what understanding or volition are in God, if we had not experienced them in ourselves. Edwards believes that a person naturally, habitually, instantaneously, and insensibly substitutes himself in place of the other in all matters of conscience and he 'easily and quietly sees whether he being in his place should approve or condemn, be angry or pleased as he is' (p. 592).

In summary, Edwards says that natural conscience consists of two things. The first is the disposition to approve or disapprove our moral treatment of others according as we are easy or uneasy in the consciousness of being consistent or inconsistent with ourselves. We have a disposition to approve our own conduct in relation to the other when we are aware of treating him as we should expect to be treated by him if he were in our case and we in his. The same holds for disapproval.

Secondly, there is, Edwards claims, another component in natural conscience which makes its appearance when we ask: What is the foundation for the approving or disapproving from uneasiness about consistency and inconsistency with ourselves? His answer is that some other grounds are needed and he finds them in the sense of *desert* (which he sometimes calls justice) or a natural proportion and harmony between malevolence and punishment, on the one hand, and loving and being loved, on the other. When a man's conscience, says Edwards, disapproves of the way he has treated his neighbour, he is in the first place aware that were he in his neighbour's position, he would resent such treatment from a sense of justice. Following on this awareness is the perception that he is not consistent with himself in doing what he would himself resent in that case. In short, approval and disapproval of conscience requires desert and justice as a ground for determining the consistency or inconsistency of the self.

It is noteworthy that Edwards makes a point of asking in what respect the natural conscience 'extends to true virtue'. His response is that conscience does not 'taste' of the primary beauty, or union of heart to Being in general, but it may approve of it 'from that uniformity, equality and justice which there is in it, and the demerit which is seen in the contrary' (p. 594). Thus, Edwards concludes, by natural conscience men 'may see the justice . . . there is in yielding all to God, as we receive all from God' (pp. 594–5). Natural conscience will approve of true virtue and disapprove the want of it, 'and yet without seeing the true beauty of it'. In the end, conscience falls short of being the exercise of a virtuous principle of the heart, and yet Edwards insists that it belongs to God's design that conscience should approve and condemn the same things approved and condemned by a spiritual sense.

The fourth and final ingredient in common morality is what Edwards calls 'instinctual kind affections' which 'in some respects resemble virtue' (p. 600). By 'instinctual' he means dispositions determining through natural laws our affections and actions toward particular objects. The purpose of these instincts in the divine economy is said to be two-fold; first, for the preservation of mankind, and, second, to promote a comfortable subsistence in the world. Certain instincts, says Edwards, of a mental and social type are 'kind affections' and have a 'semblance' of benevolence in them. However, anticipating his claim in the next section, Edwards goes on to say 'Yet . . . none of them can be of the nature of true virtue'. Edwards begins with the mutual love between parents and children which, on his view, may be understood either as natural instincts or as based on self-love; he sees no issue involved and leaves the matter there. But instead of proceeding through his list of instinctual affections, Edwards offers two reasons why they do not qualify as true virtue. We are now familiar with the basis of his claim. These affections do not arise from a principle of virtue or the union of the heart to Being in general, and, since they do not stem from general benevolence, they 'have no tendency to produce it'. In other words, according to Edwards, there is no way to reach general benevolence starting with a limited or, as he sometimes puts it, a 'private' affection limited merely to particular objects.

Edwards continues the discussion by citing affectionate relations between men and women—and expresses his agreement with Hutcheson and David Hume (1757–1838) in the view that there is a foundation in nature for these affections and that they are different from sensitive pleasure because there is in them a mutual benevolence and complacence that are not naturally 'connected with any sensitive desires' (p. 604).[19] These affections, however, are limited to opposite sexes and thus stem from a particular instinct which limits them in comparison with the principle of general benevolence which tends to no limits.

Edwards next considers pity, normally exercised toward those in calamity and having a more universal scope than the relations between the sexes. Pity, however, may be malevolent while still limited in scope, so that if the calamity of the other goes beyond the ill will one intended toward him, the natural instinct of pity comes into play. What Edwards has in mind is the case where one says 'I admit that I wished his venture would fail, but not that his life should be altogether ruined'. Even the malevolent one takes pity on the excessive character of the result.

Although Edwards is fully aware of the important role played by the morality of natural principles in furthering human life and in enhancing its quality, he is at pains to explain why these virtues have been mistaken for true virtue and why the two can never be the same. Stated most abstractly, the crucial difference between natural principles and true virtue for Edwards is the difference between limited virtues and the unlimited character of consent to Being in general. Nevertheless, there must be some resemblances between the two if we are to account for the fact that people confuse them. There is, says Edwards, something of the 'general nature of virtue' in the instinctive affections, something of the appearance of love.[20] The resemblance, however, can be misleading and Edwards intersperses in his analysis of these affections four more reasons why they are mistaken for true virtue.

People, says Edwards, take private affections for true virtue because they leave the Divine Being out of view. In failing to conceive of God as a real existent, they limit their view to a small part of the cosmic system. They think of God as 'a kind of shadowy, imaginary being' (p. 611) and while most admit that there is a God, 'yet in their ordinary view of things, his being is not apt to come into the account, and to have the influence and effect of a real existence'. The result is that we 'limit our consideration [of the beauty of affections and actions] to only a small part of the created system' (ibid.).

Another reason why people are misled in their estimate of instinctive affections is that, on Edwards's view, there 'is a true *negative* moral goodness in them' (p. 613). By this he means the negation or absence of true moral evil. A being without the natural virtues would be evidence of a much greater moral evil. The exercise of natural conscience, for example, is an evidence of the absence of that higher degree of wickedness that leads to insensibility or stupidity of conscience.[21] Thus Edwards is fully cognizant of the important role played by instinctive affections and natural virtues, at the same time he is engaged in showing why they must not be mistaken for true virtue. His recognition of the contribution made by the natural affections becomes clear when he shows concern over the fact that their power may be greatly *diminished* by pride and sensuality, the two cardinal vices strongly decried by Edwards in the Charity sermons. Since God has implanted natural principles for the well-being of mankind, their corruption can only mean the increase of evil in the world.

There is, says Edwards, yet another reason why natural principles are mistaken for true virtue and that is in their having 'in several ways' the same effect to which true virtue tends. Natural pity, gratitude, parental affections tend to the good of mankind and thus agree with the tendency of general benevolence. But then, Edwards continues, natural hunger and thirst also tend in the same direction, and 'nobody will assert that these have the nature of true virtue' (p. 616). Natural principles have the same effect as true virtue in that they tend to constrain vice and curtail wickedness. Pity delivers us from cruelty and natural conscience restrains sin. In short, for Edwards the self-love involved in these virtues plays its part in the divine economy, but it is not of the nature of true virtue, being instead a source of the world's wickedness.

Edwards's final reason why the inferior affections are taken for true virtue reveals his concern for language; some of these virtues have the same *names* as truly virtuous affections. There is, for example, a virtuous *pity* or compassion from holy benevolence that would be sufficient to excite pity to someone in calamity, even if there were no instinct determining the mind. There is also a holy *gratitude* that arises not from self-love but from a disinterested benevolence, just as there is a virtuous love of *justice* that arises from benevolence to Being in general and differs from the justice based only on what Edwards has been calling secondary beauty.[22]

We may conclude this much condensed account of Edwards's conception of true virtue and common morality with a suggestion that may serve to clarify the entire discussion. Students of the history of religion, and not only Western religion, are aware of the need to distinguish between religion and morality, between the fundamental faith in and relation to God—our *being*—and the obligations to others we have as moral beings—what we are to *do*. The distinction, but also the relation, between the two is admirably expressed in the first epistle of John, 'If a man say, I love God, and hateth his brother, he is a liar' (1 John 4:20). The love of God defines the relation to the neighbour; in biblical religion, morality is based on religion. The distinction, moreover, is not merely analytical, because time and again a tension, if not an open antagonism, has manifested itself between the two within religious traditions. Religion sees the person for whom morality is enough as a 'mere moralist' who fails to see the need of religious faith and grace; morality sees the religious person as one who depends on 'supernatural' powers and takes what William James called 'moral holidays', firm in the conviction that in God all evil is already overcome.[23] This picture is, of course, oversimplified, but it does serve to underline the problem.

According to this pattern, we could understand Edwards's account of true virtue as essentially defining the *religious* relationship, or, in his terms, the consent to and union of heart with Being in general, or the holy love of God, and his account of the relations between persons as defining the *moral* dimension, or what affections we are to have and what actions we must perform. The two sources of morality could then be understood as, on the one hand, the morality based on Christian principles, and, on the other, the morality based on natural principles stemming from the reason and order both in ourselves and the world according to the divine economy. In this way some confusion can be avoided, since 'true *virtue*' may seem to point to the *moral* dimension, whereas it is clear that, in using this expression, Edwards means the *religious* relationship to God, and its consequences.[24]

Notes

1 The reader should consult *Ethical Writings*, ed. Paul Ramsey, *The Works of Jonathan Edwards* 8 (New Haven and London: Yale University Press, 1989). This is the first complete and critical edition of these writings and the volume also contains references to most of Edwards's other works, including the 'Miscellanies', which illuminate the basic ethical writings. Ramsey's detailed Introduction is invaluable for a proper understanding of Edwards's thought about these essential topics. All references are to this edition.

2 The reader should note that the second Dissertation has been published alone with the title *The Nature of True Virtue*, ed. with an Introduction by William K. Frankena (Ann Arbor: University of Michigan Press, 1960, reprinted 1969).

3 *Ethical Writings*, p. 131.

4 *Charity* Sermon 7, 'Charity Contrary to a Selfish Spirit', *Ethical Writings*,

p. 254. The point is made even more forcefully further along in this sermon when Edwards distinguishes between self-love and 'inordinate' self-love which is selfishness; he writes, 'But I apprehend that a self-love in this sense is no fruit of the Fall, but is necessary and what belongs to that nature of all intelligent creatures which the Creator hath made . . .' (ibid., p. 255).

5 Ramsey is very helpful on this point and shows that Edwards uses the term 'grateful' in an older sense; for example, 'his coming was very grateful unto the king', conveying the sense that it was agreeable, pleasing and welcome. The important point is that, for Edwards, there is something in the nature of the thing or situation that, when *perceived*, calls for the appropriate response. See *Ethical Writings*, p. 13 n. 4.

6 *Ethical Writings*, p. 17; the 'Miscellany' is no. 530.

7 Hutcheson's main works were *An Essay on the Nature and Conduct of the Passions and the Affections* (1728) and *An Inquiry into the Original of our Ideas of Beauty and Virtue* (1725). Edwards made extensive use of both writings.

8 One is reminded here, and perhaps Edwards had this in mind himself, of the crucial distinction between *homoousios*—the same—and *homoiousios*—the similar—which played so great a role in the discussions that resulted in the formulation of the Nicene Creed. The 'orthodox' position insisted that the Son is of the *same* substance with the Father, while the 'heterodox' position claimed that the Son is of a *similar* substance with the Father. It is curious how recondite matters often find their way into ordinary language; when we say 'I do not see one iota of difference between X and Y', the meaning derives from the two Greek terms noted above. But, of course, the difference was in just that *iota*!

9 A fine illustration of the point is found in *Charity* where Edwards asks his hearers to decide whether 'you are essentially distinguished and different in your spirit from the *mere moralist*, or the heathen sage or philosopher', and whether you have 'a spirit of special esteem for and delight in these virtues that do especially belong to the gospel'. See *Ethical Writings*, p. 89.

10 See Roland A. Delattre, *Beauty and Sensibility in the Thought of Jonathan Edwards* (New Haven and London: Yale University Press, 1968). Delattre's subtitle, 'An Essay in *Aesthetics* and *Theological Ethics*' (italics added in subtitle), highlights the connection between beauty and virtue.

11 Since there are more details in Edwards's account than can be treated in a brief survey, mention must be made of an important distinction that he presupposed throughout between *benevolence* and *complacence*, both of which are included in Christian love. Referring to love going out to others, Edwards writes: 'as it respects the good enjoyed or to be enjoyed *by* the beloved, it is called *love of benevolence*; and as it respects good to be enjoyed *in* the beloved, it is called *love of complacence*' (*Charity*, pp. 212–13). For the derivation of 'complacence', including its numerous spellings, and its basic meaning of 'to be pleased in', see Eric Partridge, *Origins: A Short Etymological Dictionary of Modern English* (New York: Macmillan/London: Routledge & Kegan Paul, 1958; 2nd edn, 1959), p. 503, para. 9.

12 Edwards clearly regarded benevolence as superior to complacence and

hence it was important for him to insist that any enjoyment *in* the beloved be based on concern for the good enjoyed *by* the beloved.

13 The above is the title of ch. VII in *True Virtue*.

14 Edwards is clearly reviving the ancient doctrine of the Greek philosophers according to which every one and every thing has a proper place (*topos*) in the cosmic order so that when one is 'out of place' this can only mean that he is in someone else's place and this is unjust.

15 William Wollaston, *The Religion of Nature Delineated* (London, 1722).

16 See *Ethical Writings*, p. 570, n. 1.

17 Despite the fact that, as Ramsey correctly notes, Edwards never provided an extended discussion of the idea of a moral sense—an idea that figures prominently in the writings of eighteenth-century British moralists such as Francis Hutcheson—he introduced it in the discussion of self-love and returned to it again in connection with the next ingredient in common morality, conscience. The topic, however, is too involved to be treated here; the reader should see *Ethical Writings*, Appendix II, pp. 689–705, and Norman Fiering, *Jonathan Edwards' Moral Thought and Its British Context* (Chapel Hill: University of North Carolina Press, 1981).

18 *Ethical Writings*, p. 591, n. 5.

19 See *Ethical Writings*, p. 603 n. 9 and p. 604 n. 1 for relevant quotations from both Hutcheson and Hume.

20 It is important to notice that 'appearance' here does not mean a contrast with reality, as when one says that a person only 'appears to be honest, but is not really honest'. The meaning in Edwards's text is that the resemblance in question is present and makes its appearance in fact.

21 Edwards frequently speaks of 'stupidity' of conscience as opposed to conscience as well informed; this is a sign that he recognized the *scientia* in conscience or a knowledge of principles and norms. The familiar figure of conscience as a 'voice' has done much to make it into an intuitive, infallible oracle that simply 'tells' us what to do. For Edwards, on the contrary, there is a *judgement* of conscience based on moral knowledge.

22 Edwards spells out at greater length the role played by language in the analysis of morality. See ch. VIII in *True Virtue*, *Ethical Writings*, pp. 619–27.

23 See n. 9 above, where Edwards explicitly distinguishes between the 'mere moralist' or the 'heathen sage' and a 'spirit of special esteem for' the virtues that belong to the Gospel.

24 Once again, we see the role played by language; in the tradition of Western moral philosophy from Plato and Aristotle to the British moralists Edwards had read, the term 'virtue' signified a basically *moral* category, but by adding the term 'true' Edwards was referring to religion.

7

History and the work of redemption

When he was called in 1757 to be President of what was then the College of New Jersey, later Princeton University, Edwards wrote to the Trustees expressing concern about whether, if he accepted the post, he would have sufficient time to complete some projects upon which he had been working.[1] Chief among these projects was the *History of the Work of Redemption*, and Edwards's description of it is especially noteworthy. It represents, he writes, 'an entire new method' in divinity, since it is 'thrown into the form of a history'. Thus far, Edwards's writings took the form of treatises some of which were developed from sermons, and sermons he published in his lifetime. Edwards now had a new medium that was neither sermon nor treatise, but a narrative history meant to chart the course of redemption from the fall of man to the end of the world. His major work in this new body of divinity is the *History of Redemption*, but it is related to his earlier work, *End of Creation*.[2]

The *History of Redemption*, a work not published in Edwards's lifetime, first appeared at Edinburgh in 1774 under the supervision of John Erskine, one of Edwards's devoted friends and correspondents in Scotland. The work consists of 30 sermons all of which are on the same text from Isaiah 51:8, 'For the moth shall eat them up like a garment, and the worm shall eat them like wool: but my righteousness shall be forever, and my salvation from generation to generation'. Appended to each sermon is the same Doctrine: 'The Work of Redemption is a work that God carries on from the fall of man to the end of the world'.

There is evidence, notably from the *Miscellanies* and notebooks in which Edwards laid out the plan of the work, that he had been developing the main ideas expressed in his narrative for some time. During his ministry in Stockbridge (1750–57), after he had been dismissed from

Northampton, he indicated his need for more knowledge of Christian history, particularly the early period of the Western churches and the history of the Popes prior to the Reformation. As Wilson has pointed out, Edwards had three main sources in constructing the history of redemption; first, the Old Testament accounts of the creation of the world, the fall of mankind, the calling of Abraham and God's special relation to Israel, together with the New Testament accounts of Christ's coming and events in the early churches; second, the prophetic writings of the Old Testament, many of which Edwards interpreted as a foreshadowing of later events within the Christian Church and of external developments such as the power attained by the Bishop of Rome and the rise of Islam; third, secular or 'profane' historical literature dealing with events not recorded in sacred history.[3]

Edwards has a remarkable interpretation of the relation between these sources. In Sermon 10, after indicating that Scripture gives an account of the events in the work of redemption in two ways, that of *history* and that of *prophecy*, Edwards expresses concern that the Scripture is quite detailed in its treatment of the first five of his historical periods (see below)—the time beginning with the Fall and ending with the Babylonian captivity— but that his sixth period—from the captivity to the coming of Christ—is 'so much less the subject of Scripture history' (p. 242) than the preceding periods. His explanation of the discrepancy is the providence of God who saw to it 'that there should be authentic and full accounts of the events of this period preserved in profane history' (p. 243). Edwards, in fact, sees a clear alternation between Scripture history and profane history; the periods from the beginning to the Babylonian captivity are said to be covered by Scripture, but 'profane history gives us no account . . . of them' (ibid.). Edwards sees God's providence intimately involved in historiography; God took care that there should be a historical account of former ages not touched upon by profane history, and before profane history 'related things with some certainty', God resorted to prophecy so that by comparing those prophecies with profane history we would be able to see the agreement between the two.[4] God's design, in short, was that there should be an 'authentic' profane history as the basis for judging prophecy instead of the uncertain accounts that make up what Edwards called 'fabulous' history.

It was important for Edwards to make clear at the outset what he understood by the 'Work of Redemption' and the course of history through which it is accomplished. According to Edwards, the generations of mankind on earth did not begin until the Fall and they will continue until the end of the world; the procession of mankind is thus bounded by a beginning in the Fall and by an end in the Day of

Judgement. The entire history that ultimately connects these two events manifests God's design and its outworking in a temporal drama which has the creation for its stage. In Sermon 1, Edwards turns at once to the two senses in which the Work of Redemption can be understood. There is first a 'limited sense' in which it means the purchase of salvation, begun with Christ's incarnation, carried on during his life, and finished with his death and resurrection. In this sense, the Work, as Edwards says, 'was not so long a-doing' (p. 117), but, he continues, although the purchase of salvation was finished, 'the work itself and all that appertained to it was *virtually* done and finished but not *actually*' (ibid., italics added). We are thus led to a second and broader sense of the Work which makes it clear that Edwards did not regard God's work as taking place in some timeless realm, but as a series of events in a real history. In the broader sense the Work includes *all* that God accomplished leading up to Christ, plus the 'application' of Christ's work for the completion of God's design through the work of the Holy Spirit in history.

How seriously Edwards took the actual historical development after the work of Christ can be seen in the important distinction he made between God's work in converting souls and his work in 'the grand design in general as it relates to the universal subject and end of it' (p. 121). In the first case, God works by 'repeating after continually working the same work over again, though in different persons . . .'. That is, the work of justification and sanctification in the lives of individuals is the same age after age. With respect to the grand design, however, which includes not only individuals but the Church, nations and the social and political structures of world history, God works 'in a different manner'. It is, Edwards writes, 'not merely by the repeating and renewing the same effect on the different subjects of it that God realizes his design, but by many successive works and dispensations of God, all tending to one great aim and effect, all united as the several parts of a scheme, and altogether making up one great work' (ibid.). Edwards compares the process to the building of a house or a temple; all proceeds according to an orderly plan from the gathering of the workers and the material to the placing of the topstone. In order to consolidate the point, Edwards repeats his conception of the two ways in which God works and underlines the difference. God's effect on persons who are redeemed is an effect that is common to all ages, but with respect to the Church of God and the grand design, 'it is carried on not only by that which is common to all ages [but] by successive works wrought in different ages, all parts of one whole or one great scheme whereby one work is brought about by various steps, one step in each age and another in another' (p. 122).

Here we can see that Edwards had a clear sense of the dynamic of history wherein God acts not only by repeating past effects, but by new and successive works in different ages; God knows the grand design 'all at once', as it were, but its actualization is in the course of history, or the unfolding of time. It is in this sense that we can say that Edwards was a century ahead of his time in his understanding of the historical order, for that sense of history did not make its appearance until the nineteenth century.

Edwards had more than one scheme for arranging the periods in the history of redemption, but the picture is too complex to be treated in detail. The grand three-fold division did not change, although Edwards made some modifications in the subdivisions. The grand division runs (1) from the Fall of mankind to the coming of Christ; (2) the incarnation of Christ; (3) from Christ's resurrection to the end of the world. This is, as it were, the basic containing framework for God's design.

In Sermon 10 Edwards divides the period from the Fall to the coming of Christ into six periods as follows: 1. From the Fall to the flood; 2. From the flood to the calling of Abraham; 3. From Abraham to the redemption from Egypt; 4. From the deliverance from Egypt to the anointing of David; 5. From David's reign to the Babylonian captivity; 6. From the captivity to the coming of Christ. As is obvious, these periods represent the history of God's relation to Israel for which Edwards could rely on the Old Testament for the most part as his main source. Likewise he could rely on the New Testament writings for the appearance, life, death and resurrection of Christ. For the third period—from the resurrection to the end of the world—Edwards had a seven-fold periodization which was the result of a later revision with a new organization.

The divisions within this third period are especially noteworthy because they reveal Edwards's own excursion into the writing of history, not, of course, in the sense that he was simply 'inventing' history, but with respect to the times and movements he selected as the crucial points in God's work. The divisions are as follows: 1. The work begun at Pentecost, the outpouring of the Spirit—'this is that of which the prophet Joel hath spoken'; 2. The destruction of Jerusalem; 3. The destruction of the 'heathen empire' in Constantine's time; 4. The Reformation; 5. The fall of Antichrist; 6. The overthrow of Judaism, Islam and heathenism; 7. The consummation of the end of the world.[5] For the materials for this history, Edwards was, of course, dependent on the record of secular historians but supplemented by biblical prophecy contained in the book of Daniel and the Apocalypse.[6]

It is beyond the scope of this study to attempt any recounting of the historical development which Edwards traced through 30, often long, sermons. Moreover, such a review is not necessary since the main outline is well known from both the biblical record and the work of subsequent historians who have studied the events of the ancient world and what had happened up to the time of Edwards. Of greater value for understanding Edwards's view of God's work in redemption is a selection of examples that show his reading of the divine purpose in certain crucial events that pointed beyond themselves to some future development whose meaning could not be discerned when these events took place.

As a first example, let us consider what Edwards does with the calling of Abraham. In Sermon 4, he says that Abraham was called out of his own country to go to Canaan because God 'saw it necessary in order to the upholding of the true religion in the world that there should be a family separated from the rest of the world' (p. 158) and the corruption in it. Edwards applies the point directly to Christ; Abraham, 'that person of whom Christ was to come', and his family were separated from the rest of the world 'that his church might be upheld in his family and posterity till Christ should come'. 'This was a new thing', says Edwards, 'God had never taken any such method before.' The novelty in this approach is made clear by comparison with God's method at the time of the flood; since at that time there was no separation of God's people from the rest of the world, corruption entered through intermarriage. God's method then was to save the Church in the ark and drown the wicked world; after Abraham, God adopted a new way: instead of destroying the wicked he called Abraham and his people to live separate from the rest of the world. The people of Abraham and ultimately the Israelite nation, became a 'type' of the Church of Christ, a foundation for sustaining the Church in the world until Christ's coming.[7]

Another example of Edwards's interpretation of biblical history as it pertains to the work of redemption through the coming of Christ is found in Sermon 11 which has to do with the dispersion of the Jews after the fall of Jerusalem to the Babylonians in 586 BCE. In Esther's time, Edwards writes, 'the Jews were a people that were dispersed throughout all parts of the vast Persian empire that extended from India to Ethiopia . . .' (p. 256) and so they continued until the time of Christ. Edwards cites four ways in which the Diaspora prepared the way for Christ's coming and the founding of his kingdom in the world. The first of these was the raising throughout the world of a general expectation of a messiah to come, very near the time when he actually came. In carrying their Scriptures with them wherever they went, the Jews made known to the nations in which they lived their expectation of a glorious messiah. Edwards, following a tradition among Christian thinkers, took note of Virgil's poem about the expectation of a great prince who would institute a time of peace and righteousness, and, Edwards adds, 'some of it very much in the language of the prophet Isaiah' (p. 257).

A second contribution made by the Diaspora is that it showed the need to abolish the old dispensation and introduce the new one—the covenant of grace. It also showed the need to abolish the old ceremonial law, not least because it was virtually impossible to maintain the old Jewish worship since many Jews lived more 'than a thousand miles distant' from Judea when Christ came. A third way in which the dispersion of the Jews prepared the way for Christ is that it made known throughout the world the facts concerning Christ and his kingdom. Here Edwards reasons that, since many Jews went to Jerusalem for the three great feasts, they could not fail to learn of the wonders Christ performed there which in turn they were able to make known in the countries to which they returned. And this is not all the captivity accomplished; in Edwards's view, the dispersed Jews opened the door for the apostles to preach the Gospel because wherever they went they found synagogues where the Scriptures were read and this afforded them a place for their preaching, with the result that the new doctrine became known to the Gentiles.

Edwards finds noteworthy another important result of the dispersion, but in a different vein. During the captivity two significant additions were made to the Scripture canon—the prophecies of Ezekiel and Daniel. Their importance, according to Edwards, rests in accounts of the appearance of Christ to both of them 'in the form of that nature that he was soon to take upon him' (p. 260).[8] Here we have a very good example of what Edwards meant by his claim that the Scripture informs us through *prophecy* as well as through history. That history, however, is not to be eclipsed, can be seen in Edwards's turning at once to the overthrow of the Chaldean empire by Cyrus, and the return of the Jews to their homeland to rebuild the temple. 'This return of the Jews out of the Babylonish captivity is, next to the redemption out of Egypt, the most remarkable of all the Old Testament redemptions' (p. 263). In the clause that Edwards adds at this point, we can see clearly the meaning of typology; the return of the Jews is 'most insisted on in Scripture as a *type* of the great redemption of Jesus Christ' (ibid., italics added). The deliverance from Babylon stands for itself as a redemptive event in history, while at the same time it foreshadows a later event that is the fulfilment of all redemptions.

In Sermon 12, Edwards pursues the later history of the ancient world before Christ with the help of biblical history, profane history and the visions of Daniel, and comes finally to the conquest of the world by Alexander. For Edwards, the establishment of the 'Grecian empire' played an enormous part in furthering the work of redemption. Of all the overturnings in the world at the time, says Edwards, there occurred something which 'did remarkably promote the Work of Redemption' (p. 272) and that was the making of the Greek language *common* in the world. Thus was enhanced the spread of the Gospel from nation to nation so that, as Edwards notes, the churches at Jerusalem, Antioch, Galatia, Corinth and others could communicate with each other through this common language as recorded in the Book of Acts, something they could not have done if each had a distinct tongue. Here Edwards shows himself to be remarkably 'modern' in his approach to history; history, as G.M. Trevelyan and others were to argue almost two centuries later, is not to be confined to rulers and empires, politics and power, but must include arts and sciences, language and communication, manners and morals, dress and food, all of which conspire to make up the actual historical scene.

Edwards presses his point about the common language further and cites the translation—'about fifty or sixty years before Alexander conquered the world'—of the Old Testament into Greek—the Septuagint—and notes that the texts could now be 'understood by the Gentiles' and were no longer locked up in Hebrew 'understood by no other nation' but the Jews. Thus this development further prepared the way for Christ in that the apostles could use the Old Testament writings, especially the prophecies about Christ, in their preaching to the Gentiles.[9]

The next event in Edwards's historical odyssey is the destruction of the Grecian and the establishment of the Roman empire—'the greatest and largest temporal monarchy that ever was in the world' (p. 276). Edwards regards this development as of great importance, because when Christ came the nations were united in this one monarchy, a fact that facilitated the work of the apostles in spreading the Gospel and establishing Christ's kingdom in the world.[10]

Edwards makes much of the flourishing of learning and philosophy in the period between the captivity and the Graeco-Roman world. He concedes that there were men of 'great temporal wisdom' in this period, and it is interesting in the extreme that, while as we know, there was much emphasis by philosophers on questions about the physical world, its origin and extent, Edwards sees them as chiefly concerned with the key to human happiness. In short, it was the 'moralists' and not the 'naturalists' who occupied his attention. These philosophers, according to Edwards, had several hundred different views about happiness and thus wandered in the dark, but not altogether in vain since God thought it good to have human wisdom do its utmost before he sent the one who alone could lead the way to true happiness. The world was not becoming wiser or happier because of this wisdom, but God's plan was to show the futility of even the highest human wisdom so that the necessity of a divine teacher would become evident. This is the wisdom, says Edwards, that God made foolish, in order that men might be saved by the preaching of foolishness, that is, the Gospel that appears as 'foolishness' in the eyes of the wise.

This discussion, however, has a coda that is highly important for

Edwards's entire outlook: God has shown the vanity of human learning when it is meant to take the place of the Gospel, but 'God was pleased to make it subservient to the purposes of Christ's kingdom as an handmaid to divine revelation' (p. 278). Thus Paul was able to dispute with the philosophers because of his own knowledge of philosophy and to 'accommodate himself in his discourses to learned men' (p. 279). We need to remember that though Edwards has been linked with Karl Barth because of their concurrence about the utter sovereignty of God and the Word, Edwards does not share that total rejection of philosophy upon which Barth insisted. In short, Barth could find no point of contact with Edwards when the latter talked about God as Being in general.

The history of redemption continues and Edwards continues to chart its course, but as was noted above, we cannot follow the story in all its details, but must be content with significant illustrations of how Edwards viewed temporal events as contributing to the realization of God's total plan. Little escapes Edwards's notice in constructing his history. For example, in his long discussion of the 'dark period'—the absolute power of the Church of Rome or the 'Antichrist'—Edwards takes note of the twelfth-century Waldenses who separated themselves from the rest of the world in 'almost impassable' Alps, where they served God in the purity of his worship and never submitted to Rome. They bore, says Edwards, testimony against the Church of Rome, and he identifies their mountainous retreat with the place mentioned in Revelation 12:6 as the place made ready for the woman who was to be fed during the reign of Antichrist. Again, this is typology at work.

Toward the end of the dark time, says Edwards, there appeared the forerunners of the Reformation, notably John Wycliffe (*c.* 1329–84) and John Hus (*c.* 1396–1415) who, though persecuted and burned, contributed much to the events that were to come in God's campaign against the Antichrist. Edwards has, of course, now come to modern history or, as he says, to the period which 'begins with the Reformation and reaches to the present time' (p. 421). While he obviously could no longer appeal to the Scriptures for history he depended greatly on the prophetic contribution of Scripture for the interpretation of what happened since the Reformation. In Sermon 23, Edwards outlines the topics he intends to treat; a brief summary is in order. He speaks first of the Reformation itself and follows with the opposition instituted by the devil against the Reformed Churches, the success of the Gospel in various places, and finally the present state of things with respect to the Church of Christ and the success of Christ's work.

In describing the work of Martin Luther (1483–1546) in beginning the Reformation, Edwards stresses his pursuit of truth in the study of the Bible and the writings of the early Church Fathers to be used as touchstones for exposing the corruptions of the Roman Church. Edwards takes brief note of the efforts of Melanchthon (1497–1560), Zwingli (1484–1531) and Calvin (1509–64)—'one of the eminent of the reformers'—and passes quickly to the measures taken by the Pope to destroy the Reformation. These efforts failed, on Edwards's view, because the kingdom of Rome was so filled with darkness that they could do nothing. Resourceful as he ever was in finding scriptural support, Edwards writes 'The Reformed church was defended as Lot and the angels were in Sodom, by smiting the Sodomites with darkness or blindness that they could not find the door' (p. 423).

Edwards next takes note of the Council of Trent (1545–63) and the launching of the campaign well known to historians as the Counter-Reformation. His comment on this development is that instead of repenting of their deeds in the light of Luther's criticism, the Church of Rome persisted in its opposition and became more corrupt than ever. Edwards sees the hand of God in this response—'God hardened their hearts intending to destroy them' (p. 425). Here Edwards harks back to an ancient theme of the Old Testament; God makes hearts of stone in those he wants to destroy and makes blind those whom he intends to condemn.

One of the most interesting parts of Edwards's discussion concerning what he had previously listed under the heading of 'the success of the gospel in various places' is his account of the spread of the Gospel among the heathen. After speaking about the salutary influence of Protestantism in 'the empire of Muscovy' during the reign of Peter the Great (1682–1725), Edwards passes over quite abruptly to the situation in America. The American continent, says Edwards, was wholly unknown to the Christian nations 'till of latter times', and one of the consequences was that the devil had the people of America—the Indian nations—wholly within his power and out of the reach of the Gospel. Edwards, moreover, recounts a story he heard which explains why people came to America in the first place; the devil was so alarmed by the success of Christianity over the first three centuries and by the fall of the empire in Constantine's time, that he led many people from the 'other continent' to America where they would be beyond the reach of the Gospel and he could rule over them. The devil, however, was to be thwarted once again because God sent the Gospel to New England where true worship of God was established, and as Edwards says in a sentence that should delight the members of the Gideon Society, 'Great part of America is now full of Bibles' (p. 434).

Aware of how small was the propagation of the Gospel in heathen America, Edwards nevertheless saw the coming of the Gospel as one way in which divine providence was preparing the way for the glorious future of the Church and the overthrow of Satan's kingdom throughout the world. Edwards now sees the development of Christianity in America as a model of God's work in bringing about the widest possible dissemination of true religion. Indeed God had a hand in the discovery of the mariner's compass that enabled men to travel vast distances where before they did not dare to venture very far from land. After taking note of this global spread of Protestantism to the East Indies, Germany and Denmark, Edwards writes:

> Another thing that it would be ungrateful for us not to take notice of, is that remarkable pouring out of the Spirit of God which has been in this part of New England, of which we in this town have had such a share.[11]

Edwards's narrative account of the Work of Redemption is, as we have seen, primarily the odyssey of the divine Spirit in history and is thus an interpretation of the activities of individuals and of particular events in terms of the contribution they made to the accomplishment of God's grand design. At many points, however, we can see that Edwards has a secondary aim in writing the work, namely, to provide a basis for arguing that the Scripture is true or that the Christian religion really stems from God.

In Sermon 25 Edwards is concerned with the fact that the Church of God has invariably met with great opposition in the world, a fact that he believes is attested to by profane history no less than by sacred. And he regards such opposition as unparalleled; no other body of people have been so hated and persecuted. What, Edwards asks, is the reason for this hatred? He answers in two words: heathenism and popery. In short, the opposition to the Church has been made by wicked men. The reason, in turn, is that the religion of Christ is contrary to all wickedness, and it is hated because it stems from God. If, Edwards claims, the Scripture is not the word of God and the religion of Christ is no more than a pack of lies, it is not likely that the enemies of God would have so vigorously opposed it. It is a great argument, Edwards concludes, for the truth of Christ's religion that God has upheld it through so many dangers and oppositions. This favouring hand of God, says Edwards, is one of the great wonders that ever happened—'There is nothing like it up on the face of the earth . . . no other society of men that has stood as the church has done' (p. 446).

For the remainder of his account, that is, the period 'which is from the present time till the Antichrist is fallen' and Satan's visible kingdom is destroyed, Edwards is, of course, entirely dependent on biblical prophecy and he must try to project the events needed to realize God's design through the enigmatic language and imagery of the Apocalypse. Edwards is fully aware of the difficulties he faces and says that, in addition to the differences of opinion to be encountered in the interpretation of prophecy, 'we know not what particular events are to come to pass' before God overthrows the kingdom of Satan. As it turns out, our lack of knowledge of 'particular events' to come does not preclude knowing the objective to be achieved by God in the work of redemption, namely, the overthrow of the enemies of the Church.

Edwards's list of such enemies is noteworthy; there is, first, heresy, under which heading appear Socinianism and Arianism, Quakerism and Arminianism; second is the kingdom of Antichrist represented by the 'spiritual Babylon, that great city Rome', which was brought down by the Reformation but remains to be destroyed; third is the Mohammedan kingdom that is to be the target of the locusts and horsemen—Revelation 9—who will capture the false prophet and destroy him; fourth, and in many ways the most important, is the Jewish religion. Edwards does not speak of the Jews as 'enemies', but only of their 'infidelity' in rejecting Christ 'against the plain teachings of their own prophets'. In this case the work of God would be positive and not destructive: 'the national conversion of the Jews'. In all these ways the visible kingdom of Satan will be done away and the kingdom of Christ will be extended through the 'whole habitable globe'. Knowledge of God, as foreshadowed by the prophecy of Isaiah, shall cover the earth as the waters cover the sea. There will be universal peace and love, understanding among all nations and the end of war.

The work of redemption will be completed when the dead are raised, when the saints 'meet the Lord in the air', and the whole Church has been delivered from all peril. All that will happen shows the unity of God's 'whole plan'. Reason, moreover, in Edwards's view, shows that it is fitting that rational beings should have knowledge of God's scheme, 'for they doubtless are the beings that are principally concerned in it' (p. 521). Such knowledge is important for Edwards, because it is essential that rational beings should see God's glory in his works, something they could not do were they ignorant of his plan.

It is at this point that the history of redemption is essentially related to Edwards's underlying concern for God's aim in creation. The glory of God is manifest in the wonders of the creation—the order and harmony bringing into one system all creatures great and small, animate and inanimate. Nature is the stage upon which the drama of history is enacted, but just as there was needed an intelligent being, one who can appreciate God's glory in the beauty and excellency of the cosmos, so there must be a rational being who can appreciate the glory of God in the great work he has done in history. We can see here on a grand scale what

Edwards meant when he insisted, from the beginning of his thought, that 'one alone' is not excellent. The fulfilment, not the origin, of excellency is excellency *acknowledged* and appreciated by a being endowed with the power to do so. God did not need, but wanted, out of the depth of his love to have his *gloria* communicated through and to his creatures—the consent of beings to Being in general.

Having traced so long a history, Edwards offers at the end a remarkably short summary of the wisdom of God revealed in his accomplishments. In Sermon 30, we are told three things in the simplest terms. First, God created the world for the excellent use of achieving the work of redemption; second, God used the fall—'so sorrowful and deplorable'—as the means of bringing such good out of evil, and, third, the Work of Redemption is the process whereby that good has been brought about. Thus Edwards's drama of sacred history has many scenes but only three acts—Creation, Fall and Redemption—and they each point to God's glory as revealed to man.

The influence of Edwards's *History of Redemption* has been considerable, as Wilson has pointed out in his account of the subsequent appraisals and interpretations advanced from the eighteenth century to the present.[12] One of the most recent interpretations has been offered by William J. Scheick; it is instructive both for what it includes and what it fails to take into account.[13] Scheick's proposal is to understand the work as an allegory of the process of individual conversion. As Wilson points out, there is a passage in Sermon 3 which does suggest an analogy between cosmic redemption and the development within the individual soul.[14] That Edwards draws the analogy in one place, however, does not show that it is adequate for interpreting the work as a whole, and, indeed what is left out in this analogy goes to the heart of what Edwards understood by history.

The idea that the *History of Redemption* is 'an allegory of the blessed soul' runs counter to what Edwards wrote about the difference between God's activity in relation to individuals and his work in accomplishing the grand design through history.[15] Edwards is quite clear about the difference; in the case of individuals and their conversion, God is said to work by repeating the same thing in every age, but with different individuals. However, in dealing with the Church, nations and the social and political structures of world history, God, Edwards claims, works 'in a different manner'. Instead of the repetition of the same effect common to all ages as in individual conversion, God accomplishes the redemptive plan 'by successive works wrought in different ages . . . one step in each age and another in another'.

Here Edwards lays hold of an idea crucial for the very notion of history and it has a number of significant implications. To begin with,

Edwards sees that history, both as event and record, cannot be understood in terms of individuals alone. Great individuals, to be sure, have played their part in history, but even Hegel, who saw a special role for his 'world-historical individuals', still regarded the state as the chief agent in historical development. There are corporate realities to contend with—nations, societies, Churches—and, as Edwards understood so well in his interpretation of original sin, these realities are as little to be construed as 'collections' of individuals as is mankind itself.

We shall return shortly to the problem posed by *nominalism*, but first it is necessary to bring in another implication of Edwards's distinction between the two ways of God's working. While he certainly included in the work of redemption the conversion of individuals, he was just as certainly contrasting the repetition of the same event in all ages with successive works in different ages together with the idea that these works are progressive steps toward one goal. Individual conversions signal the same effect in every age, but they can be incidents in a real historical order only if there is such an order based, not on individuals alone, but on the interactions of nations, peoples, communities and Churches. In short, for Edwards, history is not possible through repetition, but requires change, development and advance to a consummation.[16]

Returning to the point about nominalism, it is essential to understand that, for all his involvement with Locke and the British philosophical tradition, Edwards was *not* a nominalist, which is to say that he did not believe that *individuals* alone exist. Miller saw this point long ago when he used as a headnote to his chapter on 'Sin' in *Jonathan Edwards* a passage from Charles Peirce in which he says that the dispute over nominalism and realism has had consequences far beyond the sphere of logic, the most important of which is that, if nominalism is true, *mankind* is no more than a fiction. Just as mankind is not the 'sum' of individuals, and original sin is not the 'sum' of individual misdoing, history is not the 'sum' of the actions of individuals but the dynamic relations between corporate entities in which there are novel developments that result in the achievement of ends.

The idea that Edwards's *History of Redemption* is an allegory of the individual soul not only runs counter to his anti-nominalism, but it leaves out of account Edwards's main point about God's two ways of working in realizing his grand design—the way of individual conversion which is the *same* in *all* ages, although the individuals are different, and the way of *successive* works brought about in *different* ages. Were only the first method available, it seems clear that there could be no *history* at all and no development of the sort needed for accomplishing the cosmic redemption, since there then would be no novelty but only the divine activity repeating itself. Even individual conversions could be said to take place 'in' history only if there were already a real historical order in place. To put the matter in another way, if the effects on individuals wrought by the divine Spirit were the only form of God's activity there could be no historical order. But, as Edwards acutely saw, there is such an order precisely because God works 'in a different manner' in dealing with the structures through which world history moves.

Miller stressed two points in connection with Edwards's conception of history, his belief that history is a unity and that there is no history without interpretation. The first point is undoubtedly correct in view of Edwards's focus on the *one* process through which the divine scheme is to be brought to fruition. The second point, however, is open to question when we consider that one of the chief complaints advanced by Pierre Bayle and Voltaire against J.B. Bossuet's *Theological Discourse on Universal History* (1681) is that it contained too much 'interpretation', by which they meant that its historical facts are based on the authority of the Bible and, ultimately, on Church authority and tradition.[17] Recognition of the need for interpretation in the recording and understanding of history certainly did not begin with Edwards, skilful as he was as an interpreter and typologist; the need for a focus, a unifying purpose, a guiding thread for the writing of history was clearly recognized in the Enlightenment.

Comparing Voltaire's historical writings with Bossuet's *Discourse*, Ernst Cassirer writes 'Just as Bossuet projected his theological ideal into history, so Voltaire projects his philosophical ideal; as the former applies to history the standard of the Bible, so the latter freely applies his rational standards to the past'.[18] Voltaire had his own tale to tell, a history of the triumph of the ideals of Enlightenment—rationality and progress—over the evils of superstition and religion. The indispensability of unifying ideas and ideals for the comprehension of history was to be further demonstrated in the nineteenth century when Hegel proposed that history is the realization of freedom and Karl Marx maintained that history is the overcoming of human alienation.

The issue, then, cannot be simply a matter of the presence or the absence of unifying ideas and purposes in the writing of history, since these are present in every history, profane as well as sacred. The problem concerns instead the selection of these ideas and that will depend in turn on the purpose of the writer and the subject-matter to be considered. As Wilson correctly points out (p. 97), Edwards was fully aware that he was writing a history of *redemption*, of the deeds whereby God is to accomplish his design through the grand divisions of the Creation, the Fall and the End of the world. We should not even say that this is a history written from a 'religious' point of view, because that would suggest an effort to write a world, 'secular' history after the fashion of a Voltaire or a

Leopold von Ranke, but with a different focus. Edwards's history is thoroughly theological and in the vein of the ancient Hebrew prophets; persons and events figure in this history not primarily as matters of historical knowledge—'what really happened in history'—but rather as means and *manifestations* of divine redemption. Edwards did not regard his account as replacing secular histories or as a substitute for them in any sense; his work represents, as he said, a 'new method in divinity' which is cast in the form of historical narrative instead of theological and philosophical discussion of the sort to be found in his great treatises.

Peter Gay, in his account of Puritan historians in colonial America, misses this point and supposes that an appraisal of Edwards's *History of Redemption* is to be based solely on a contrast between the 'empirical' history represented by a Voltaire or a Hume and Edwards's 'religious propaganda'. Such a direct comparison is not very illuminating because it fails to take into account the fundamental difference in *purpose* between what Edwards was doing and the efforts of the Enlightenment thinkers to establish a 'scientific' history.[19] Edwards was fully aware of his purpose in writing a history of *redemption*, that is, a 'sacred' and not a 'profane' history, hence if any comparison is relevant at all it should be between Edwards's *History* and Bossuet's *Discourse*, since both are of the same type. The more important point, however, is not in such comparisons, but in Edwards's conception of history itself. Edwards had a conception of a real historical order marked by change, novelty and development and in this respect Miller was right to compare him to Marx who shared that conception despite the fact that his and Edwards's interpretative structures are very far apart.

Here we must recall what was said earlier about Edwards's having distinguished between 'fabulous' and 'authentic profane history' and his concern that Scripture history does not deal with the period from the Babylonian captivity to the coming of Christ. The omission, says Edwards, is compensated for because the providence of God saw to it 'that there should be authentic and full accounts of this period preserved in profane history'. In short, Edwards fully recognized the existence and importance of profane history and he does not suppose that his history of redemption should take its place.

Previous discussions of Edwards's understanding of history have focused attention on whether he has a 'modern' view or whether he must be assigned to what is presumably a less enlightened age. The question so put is not very fruitful because of the notorious difficulty of determining the meaning of 'modern'. A more illuminating comparison would be to locate him in relation to another distinction that has found some acceptance, namely, the contrast between the view prevailing in the eighteenth century concerning history and that dominant in the nineteenth century. In the former period there was indeed a great interest in history, but it was conceived largely in terms of ideal types or a series of tableaux succeeding each other in a temporal order much like a museum exhibit devoted to tracing the history of costumes through a century. Not only is each stage static, but there is no sense of a dynamic movement from one state to the next involving development and novelty.[20]

The nineteenth century, with some help from Hegel, the new interest in natural history and ideas about evolution, saw a significant change; history was now seen as a dynamic continuum of events marked by change and novelty and accompanied by a sense of how later forms develop from earlier ones. Against this background, Edwards shows himself to be a century ahead of his time. He not only manifests this dynamic conception as we have seen in his distinction between the two ways in which God works in history, but he also carries it as far as it can go in his idea that 'heaven is a progressive state', ever reaching toward a higher perfection:

> We may judge of the end that the Creator aimed at in the being, nature and tendency he gives the creature, by the mark or term which they constantly aim at in their tendency and *eternal progress*; though the time will never come when it can be said it is attained to, in the absolutely perfect manner.[21]

Notes

1 This letter will be published subsequently in the *Letters* volumes of the *Works*, edited by George Claghorn. See *A History of the Work of Redemption*, transcribed and edited by John F. Wilson, *The Works of Jonathan Edwards* 9 (New Haven and London: Yale University Press, 1989), pp. 62–3.

2 See *A History of the Work of Redemption*, p. 69. Wilson's excellent Introduction and notes to the text are invaluable for understanding the circumstances of the composition and publication of the *History* and the unfolding of Edwards's exhaustive narrative meant to chart the events that began with 'the fall of man' and concluded with 'the end of the world'. The text of the essay, *End of Creation* . . . noted above is found in *Ethical Writings*, ed. Paul Ramsey, *The Works of Jonathan Edwards* 8 (New Haven and London; Yale University Press, 1989), pp. 403–536.

3 We must remember that, for Protestantism especially, the Old Testament was believed to contain the seeds of the Gospel; Luther described the Bible as the 'cradle of Christ' and, along with Johann Reuchlin (1455–1522), argued vigorously on behalf of retaining the study of Hebrew and the canon of the Old Testament. Hence, Edwards's use of the Jewish scriptures is the continuation of a long tradition.

4 To grasp the subtlety of this point it is necessary to take note of what Edwards knew about ancient historiography. He distinguishes between the 'fabulous age' and the 'historical age'—the beginning of 'authentic profane history'—and supposes that the latter began a century before Nebuchadnezzar's time, about 460 BCE. See *A History of the Work of Redemption*, p. 243 n. 3.

5 The seventh period is variously described by Edwards as the triumph of the Church throughout the world, the Day of Judgement, the final completion of the Work of Redemption.

6 See *Apocalyptic Writings*, ed. Stephen J. Stein, *The Works of Jonathan Edwards* 5 (New Haven and London: Yale University Press, 1977). Stein's Introduction and notes are invaluable for understanding the apocalyptic tradition, Edwards's thoughts about the Millennium, and the principles of apocalyptic interpretation he followed.

7 A brief explanation of the meaning of *typology* as a rhetorical device adopted by the Reformed traditions for interpreting the Bible, and especially the relation between the Testaments, will be helpful at this point. There was developed in the Middle Ages the idea of the four-fold senses or meanings to be found in Scripture, an idea that was adopted by Thomas Aquinas and by Nicholas of Lyra, so that it had the authority of both a great theologian and one who has come to be regarded as the foremost Christian commentator on the Scriptures up to the fourteenth century. The four senses were: 1. The 'literal' or historical, recording what was done; 2. the allegorical, where something is understood through something else; 3. the tropological, or the moral meaning; 4. the anagogical, or the leading of the mind to heavenly things, sometimes called mystical. The crucial point is that the Reformers reacted against this scheme and insisted on the primacy of the literal, especially the historical, meaning, and developed what is essentially an intra-biblical mode of interpretation or the interpretation of the Old Testament which involves taking individuals and events as 'types' and prophecies to be fulfilled in the New Testament and later history. See *A History of the Work of Redemption*, p. 43 where Wilson cites the formulation by Erich Auerbach of figural interpretation as establishing a connection between two events or persons such that the first signifies not only itself but the second as well, while the second fulfils the first. Thus Abraham's living separate from the rest of the world is a 'type' of Christ's Church in the world. Examples abound in Edwards's writings where David is a central figure—'the ancestor and great type of Christ' (p. 204). For recent literature on typology see *A History of the Work of Redemption*, p. 44, n. 8, 9.

8 The passages cited are Ezekiel 1:26 and Daniel 8:15–16, which are said to record the appearances of Christ. Many other passages are drawn by Edwards from the two prophets; all have to do with the previsioning of events yet to come.

9 The Septuagint was started in the middle of the third century BCE and nearly all of it was finished before the Christian era. Textually, this translation is of major importance because the Hebrew texts are older than standard Hebrew manuscripts, including the Massoretic text. Edwards's point about the role of the Septuagint in making the Old Testament available to the

Gentiles is still maintained by scholars today. See *The Oxford Classical Dictionary*, ed. N. G. L. Hammond and H. H. Scullard (2nd edn; Oxford: Clarendon Press, 1970), 'Septuagint', pp. 978–9.

10 See Sermon 12, *A History of the Work of Redemption*, p. 277 for Edwards's comparison of the Roman empire to the English nation; in both cases communication is said to be 'quick and easy from one part of the nation to another'.

11 *A History of the Work of Redemption*, p. 436. Edwards refers here to the revival of 1734–35 that took place in Northampton. See Chapter 3 above.

12 See *A History of the Work of Redemption*, pp. 79–100.

13 'The Grand Design: Jonathan Edwards' *History of the Work of Redemption*', *Eighteenth Century Studies* 8 (1975), pp. 300–14; repr. in *Critical Essays on Jonathan Edwards*, ed. William J. Scheick (Boston: G.K. Hall, 1980). I am indebted to John Wilson for this reference.

14 *A History of the Work of Redemption*, pp. 99.

15 See pp. 121ff. above.

16 There is an interesting parallel here with the efforts of the Enlightenment thinkers to develop their conception of history. It was thought that the underlying subject of history is human nature which does *not change*, but the histories of the time were mainly about *changing* customs and manners, and the question that arose was: Is change an illusion? The question itself suggests that no history is possible without change and development. See Ernst Cassirer, *The Philosophy of the Enlightenment*, trans. F. C. A. Koelln and J. A. Pettegrove (Boston: Beacon Press, 1955), p. 219.

17 'Interpretation' has always suffered from an ambiguity in which it is used in a pejorative sense opposed to 'fact'—'we were not given the facts, but only their interpretations'. This obscures the positive sense of the term or the need to determine the significant relevance or importance of persons and events in a discourse that is in the form of a history and not a mere chronicle of happenings and dates. It is in this sense that interpretation is essential to a history.

18 Cassirer, op. cit., p. 222.

19 Actually, the Enlightenment picture is far more complex than is suggested by an 'empirical' versus 'religious propaganda' formula, as Cassirer has shown. See Cassirer, op. cit., pp. 204–6.

20 See ibid., pp. 212–13. In commenting on Montesquieu's (1689–1755) historical method of 'ideal types', Cassirer says that they are 'purely static' forms; 'they offer a principle of explanation for the structure of the social body but they contain no means of revealing the functioning of this body'. At another point in his discussion Cassirer notes: 'The analytic spirit, which is characteristic of the eighteenth century . . . tends to stress uniformity and constancy rather than change and flux in the treatment of historical phenomena' (p. 226).

21 *Ethical Writings*, p. 535; italics added.

8

Edwards as preacher and interpreter of Scripture

We must not allow our interest in Edwards as a theologian and philosopher to overshadow his importance as a preacher and interpreter of Scripture. He was well aware of the emphasis placed by the Reformed traditions on the Bible and on the reading, preaching and interpreting of the Word.[1] In addition to his major treatises, Edwards wrote and delivered a great many sermons throughout his career as pastor, beginning with his short ministry at a small church in New York, formed by dissenters from the Presbyterian Church, and ending with his years in Northampton where he had succeeded his grandfather Solomon Stoddard as pastor. Some 1,200 sermon manuscripts have survived and it is estimated that these amount to no more than four-fifths of Edwards's actual output.[2] Only about half of these manuscripts will be published, since Edwards no longer wrote them out in full after 1742 but relied instead upon outlines containing various marks indicating what he had to supply extempore. Although the outlines are important as part of the record to be consulted by scholars, nothing would be served by publishing them in letterpress form.

In his sermons Edwards followed the pattern well established in seventeenth-century rational discourse and which he inherited from his father Timothy Edwards and his grandfather Solomon Stoddard. The pattern involves starting with the Text, moving on to the Doctrine to be 'raised' from the Text and proceeding to the Application which further develops the topic—God, sin, righteousness, etc.—in subsections, and ending with the perceptions the congregation should have about the topic plus their implications for conduct. As Kimnach has pointed out, in following this pattern over many years Edwards reveals a great deal of his own experience and development. The earliest sermons are notable for their stress on Edwards's personal religious odyssey, his meditations, thoughts and recounting the times when he had the most vivid sense of the presence of God. The sermons of his middle years are largely theological in content and pastoral in tone, while his later sermons suggest that his concern for preaching was on the wane, a result of his being distracted by the preparation of his treatises.

Edwards, for the most part, read his sermons, although there are indications that he would have liked to speak extemporaneously. It appears that he was under some pressure from Stoddard not to read his sermons, but to preach more freely. The fervour, moreover, generated during the Great Awakening called for something more dramatic than a discourse read out as if it were a treatise.[3] Edwards's effort to meet this demand may account for the fact that after 1742 he was outlining his sermons more and more. In the end, however, it appears that he was not at ease in preaching only from notes and the record shows that he was not very effective as a preacher between 1742 and his dismissal from Northampton in 1750. It is highly significant that his 'Farewell Sermon', the last he preached as official pastor in Northampton, is fully written out and that was some eight years after he began relying on outlines.

It is not surprising to find that by all accounts Edwards's talents were far more literary than oratorical. His weak points appear to have been in voice, gesture and rhythm; his great power was in his masterful use of language. As we have seen, he was meticulous in his choice of words in order to achieve the greatest accuracy in the ideas they were meant to convey and, above all, he was concerned to make these ideas 'sensible' through vivid images, metaphors and dramatic comparisons. Despite the need to keep the famous Enfield sermon, 'Sinners in the Hands of an Angry God', from exercising undue importance, there is no denying the terror of its rhetoric. The figure of the sinner suspended by nothing more than a thread of the spider's web over the fiery pit below, and held there only by the sovereign pleasure of God, is an image that no one is likely to forget. The doctrine of sin, divine wrath and punishment could indeed be expressed, in Edwards's terms, as a matter of a 'purely notional understanding', but for him that was not enough; the more that is needed is to make persons 'sensible' of what the doctrine means in their own experience.[4]

Edwards's ability to bring ideas and doctrine to life, to lead the congregation to see, feel and be affected by what they heard is confirmed many times over. Dwight informs us that one of Edwards's 'youthful auditors' told his father that he had been present when Edwards 'delivered the sermon in the History of Redemption, in which he describes the Day of Judgment; and that so vivid and solemn, was the impression made on his own mind, that he fully supposed, that, as soon as Mr. Edwards should close his discourse, the Judge would descend, and the final separation take place'.[5]

Edwards had a remarkable ability to portray the thoughts and feelings of others after the fashion of what he had described in *True Virtue* as changing places with the other in order to see the situation from the other point of view. He often used this power to goad his hearers or to awaken them to their true state. In a sermon, 'The Future Punishment of the Wicked; Unavoidable and Intolerable', Edwards begins by projecting what sinners often think when they hear of hell's torments—'. . . they sometimes think with themselves: Well, if it shall come to that, that I must go to hell, I will bear it as well as I can . . .'. Their hope, Edwards says, is that they will thus clothe themselves with resolution, but their hope is in vain, for 'the first moment they feel it [the wrath of God], their hearts will become like wax before the furnace. Their courage and resolution will all be gone in an instant; it will vanish away like a shadow in the twinkling of an eye.' Before the awesome punishment all human differences will disappear; 'the stoutest and most sturdy', he continues, 'will have no more courage than the feeblest infant: let a man be an infant, or a giant, it will be all one'.[6]

Much as Edwards believed that, in their very nature, the things of religion must be spoken about in an 'affecting' style, we are not to suppose that his preaching was, in words he used in discussing false affections, 'all heat and no light'. On the contrary, his sermons are always models of carefully reasoned discourse, a fact acknowledged even by those not entirely in sympathy with his doctrine. The issue is in any case not an opposition between affections and thought—*Religious Affections* was dedicated to overcoming any such opposition—but rather in differences of rhetorical style. In addition to painting powerful and dramatic images in his sermons, always, to be sure, for the purpose of driving home a doctrine and its applications, Edwards could adopt a stance that is best described as an invitation 'to come and reason together'. An excellent example of this approach is the sermon on John 14:27, 'Peace I leave with you, my peace I give unto you: not as the world giveth, give I unto you'. The basic idea of the sermon is simple and clear: the peace Christ offers is based on truth about ourselves, God and the world, while the worldling gains his or her peace through self-deception and a turning away from truth:

> Christ's peace is a reasonable peace and rest of soul; it is what has foundation in light and knowledge, in the proper exercises of reason, and a right view of things; whereas the peace of the world is founded in blindness and delusion. The peace that the people of

> Christ have, arises from their having their eyes open, and seeing things as they be. The more they consider, and the more they know of the truth and reality of things, the more they know what is true concerning themselves, the state and condition they are in; the more they know of God . . . the more their consciences are awakened and enlightened . . .

In drawing the main comparison, Edwards fastens on the role of reason:

> The worldly man's peace cannot be maintained but by avoiding consideration and reflection. If he allows himself to think, and properly to exercise his reason, it destroys his quietness and comfort. If he would establish his carnal peace, it concerns him to put out the light of his mind, and turn beast as fast as he can. The faculty of reason, if at liberty, proves a mortal enemy to his peace. It concerns him, if he would keep alive his peace, to contrive all ways that may be, to stupefy his mind and deceive himself, and to imagine things to be otherwise than they be.

In a parting thrust, Edwards says 'But with respect to the peace which Christ gives, reason is its great friend'.[7]

In addition to 'Sinners', by far the best known of Edwards's sermons, and the historically important 'Farewell Sermon' which he preached when he and the congregation at Northampton separated, we must take note of two other important sermons, both of which were published in Edwards's lifetime—'God Glorified in Man's Dependence',[8] and 'A Divine and Supernatural Light'. In the first of these, the famous Boston Lecture of 1731, Edwards set forth his own uncompromising position: that the redeemed are 'in every thing, directly, immediately, and entirely dependent on God . . . that the creature is nothing, and that God is all'. From this Edwards drew the corollary: God is under no obligation to save anybody, but acts only at his sovereign pleasure. In affirming this doctrine, Edwards was striking a blow at the root of what was then known as the 'Covenant or Federal theology' according to which the relation between man and God took the form of a covenant established by God so that at the time of conversion the person enters into a compact with God that guarantees security until such time as the individual has been sealed in the Spirit through the sacraments. Such an arrangement, of course, implies consent from *both sides* and Edwards saw this as an intolerable infringement on the divine sovereignty, but even more important, the covenant of Grace for Edwards is one made not between God and men, but between God and Christ. It is only through the relation to Christ that anyone enters into this covenant. As Miller has pointed out, Edwards was so emphatic on the utter dependence of man on God that he did not even argue the point: 'The Federal Theology is conspicuous in his sermon by its utter absence'.[9]

In the sermon on the divine light Edwards sets forth his own version of the doctrine of illumination which goes back to Augustine. The basic figure is clear: just as things are visible to us through their reflection of the light coming from the sun, we are able to grasp through the understanding the meaning and truth of the things of religion only through a divine light that enlightens us. The time-honoured formula was *In lumine tuo, videbimus lumen*—'In Thy light shall we see light'. Since the substance of this sermon appears in *Religious Affections* in the discussion of a spiritual understanding, there is no need to repeat the details here. Two points, however, are noteworthy in the present context. First, that the divine light is a true *sense* of the excellency—beauty—of what is contained in the Word, and as a consequence of that sense, there is a *conviction* of its truth and reality. The emphasis on having a 'sense of' this excellency is meant to contrast with a merely notional understanding: 'He that is spiritually enlightened truly apprehends, and sees it [God's glory], or has a sense of it'. Here Edwards anticipates the idea of affections which was central to his interpretation of the revivals.

Second, the manner in which the divine light is communicated to us reinforces the idea of the total sovereignty of God set forth in the previous sermon. The light is given to us immediately and that means 'that it is given by God without making use of any means that operate by their own power, or a natural force'. There are not 'truly any second causes of it; but it is produced by God immediately'. If one were to ask, given the total body of what Edwards wrote, what one idea stands out as more important than any other, the answer would have to be the utter sovereignty of God and the vehement denial of the existence of what were called 'secondary causes' or any power to operate independently of God. Edwards could thus stand with Spinoza as one of the 'God-intoxicated' men.

Behind Edwards's sermons there stands a vast body of scholarship, including Scripture commentary and interpretation, history both sacred and secular, church history and the writings of the Church Fathers, works of theology and philosophy and, not least, the religious writings of his contemporaries in New England and abroad, especially in England and Scotland. The extent of his learning is evident in the sermons themselves, but there are other sources of information concerning the subjects that interested him and the books he had read. As

Wilson Kimnach has pointed out, Edwards's sermons are connected with all of his major notebooks in which he entered the materials for his projects and outlines for carrying them out. There also exists a 'Catalogue' that has been aptly described by Stephen Stein as 'that intriguing but uncharted map of his reading' in which Edwards recorded many titles and authors together with comments and in some cases condensations of entire works, directions to himself to obtain a particular book and other kinds of entries.[10] The chief reason why Stein calls this manuscript 'uncharted' is the enigmas it poses. It is not always possible, for example, to determine whether the entry of an author or title means that Edwards was trying to obtain the book or that he has already read it. Titles crossed out could suggest either that he did find the book or that he stopped trying to do so. The resolution of these problems need not concern us here; what is important is the information contained in the 'Catalogue' about the books Edwards was able to consult in addition to those he had in his own library.

Edwards's approach to the Scriptures was philological, historical and stylistic, with great emphasis on typology as the manner of indicating the parallels between the Old and New Testaments. Although Edwards knew well enough how to find the biblical passages relevant to a particular theme or argument, he was not one to suppose that these texts might be made to mean anything you please or that their meaning could be determined by anything less than a careful and disciplined study through the original languages of the texts themselves. He had no sympathy with those who believed that they had the meaning of biblical passages and incidents communicated to them immediately through visions or sudden insights generally associated with 'enthusiasm'. On the contrary, he had what might be called a 'realistic' sense of meaning; Scripture contains the divine Word and its meaning is there to be understood but only through exact scholarship. Edwards had command of Latin, Greek and Hebrew, as all his notebooks show and also his entries in the 'Blank Bible'. In quoting from Calvin's *Institutes*, for example, he usually made his own translations from the Latin text and his exegesis of biblical passages shows his knowledge of Greek, including the Septuagint, and he was well equipped to deal with the subtleties of Hebrew syntax.

As an indication of the comprehensiveness with which he approached his projects, consider the following list of topics, noted as 'Books to be Inquired for', he thought necessary for his work on the Apocalypse (he had drawn up a similar list in preparation for the *History of Redemption*):

The best geography
The best history of the world
The best exposition of the Apocalypse
The best general ecclesiastical history from Christ to the present time
The best upon the Types of the Scripture
Which are the most useful and necessary of the Fathers
The best chronology
The best historical dictionary of the nature of a Bayle's dictionary
The best that treats of the cabalistical learning of the Jews[11]

Countless examples could be given of Edwards's ability and perceptiveness in the use of the biblical languages; I choose a typical instance, one taken from the *Humble Attempt* and which involves Hebrew language structure.[12] He has been outlining various aspects of the proposal for extraordinary prayer, the duty to do it, the good to come of the concert, the nature of the union to be achieved, and he ends with the 'manner of prayer' the meaning of which is best conveyed through his own words rather than in any abstract description:

> We may observe the *manner of prayer* agreed on . . . 'Let us go speedily to pray' (Zech. 8:21); or as it is in the margin, 'Let us go continually.' The words literally translated are, 'Let us go in going.' Such an ingemination [i.e., repetition] or doubling of words is very common in the Hebrew language, when it is intended that a thing shall be very strongly expressed; it generally implies the superlative degree of a thing; as the 'Holy of Holies' signifies the most holy . . . [13]

He then goes on to explain the matter more fully:

> . . . as this ingemination of words in the Hebrew, in general denotes the strength of expression, so it is used to signify almost all those things that are wont to be signified by the various forms of strong speech in other languages . . . [14]

That this is no mere display of learning on Edwards's part becomes clear when he tells us that the Hebrew form of expression 'represents the earnestness of those that make the proposal, their great engagedness in the affair . . . that they should be speedy, fervent, and constant in it; or, in one word, that it should be thoroughly performed'.

It should now be clear that Edwards the preacher and Edwards the interpreter of Scripture go hand in hand. He used his scholarly abilities to the utmost in uncovering the meaning of biblical texts, firm in the belief that the word he spoke was not an expression of his own private and personal opinion but the result of the most exacting study of the Bible where, as he had written in the *Personal Narrative*, 'I seemed often to see so much light exhibited by every sentence, and such a refreshing food communicated, that I could not get along in reading; often dwelling long on one sentence . . .'.

Notes

1 The following entry in his *Diary*, for Saturday, 23 May 1724, is revealing in this connection: 'How it comes about I know not, but I have remarked it hitherto, that at those times, when I have read the Scriptures most, I have evermore been more lively and in the best frame'. In his *Personal Narrative*, Edwards wrote: 'I had then, and at other times, the greatest delight in the holy scriptures, of any book whatsoever. Oftentimes in reading it, every word seemed to touch my heart. I felt a harmony between something in my heart, and those sweet and powerful words. I seemed often to see so much light exhibited by every sentence, and such a refreshing food communicated, that I could not get along in reading; often dwelling long on one sentence, to see the wonders contained in it; and yet almost every sentence seemed to be full of wonders.'

2 A small number of sermons were published in Edwards's lifetime, notably 'God Glorified in Man's Dependence' and 'A Divine and Supernatural Light', and some have appeared in earlier editions of his *Works*. The bulk of these manuscripts, however, are as yet unpublished, but their transcription and editing are going forward under the supervision of Wilson Kimnach, editor for the *Sermons* in the Yale edition. Kimnach, with the help of Thomas A. Schafer, editor for the *Miscellanies* and the first to date these entries, has been able to establish a chronology for the sermons and they are to be published in chronological order according to the period they cover in Edwards's life. The first volume, *The New York Period*, consisting of Edwards's earliest sermons, is currently in press. I am indebted to Kimnach for his work in analysing the structure of all of the sermons and in placing Edwards in the context of Puritan preaching. The reader should consult Kimnach's comprehensive Introduction to the first volume of *Sermons* in the Yale edition.

3 The line between sermon and treatise, as Kimnach has suggested, is more difficult to draw than might be thought. The *Treatise Concerning Religious Affections*, for example, was said to have been composed of sermons Edwards had preached from his pulpit and the same holds true for the *History of Redemption*. Dwight took note of the connection in his discussion of Edwards as a preacher. 'He preached extensively', he wrote, 'on subjects, continued through a series of discourses; many of his Treatises having been a course of sermons actually delivered from the desk' (Sereno Edwards Dwight, *Life of President Edwards* (1830), p. 601). There is no good reason to question Dwight's claim, but this does not mean that Edwards did not rework sermons into treatise form. *Religious Affections*, for example, begins with a biblical text, 1 Peter 1:8, 'Whom having not seen, ye love . . .', and the first Part of the work has the typical

sermon structure. In Parts Two and Three, however, this structure is less evident and the discussion becomes more analytical, suggesting that he had turned it into a treatise, hence the full title *A Treatise Concerning Religious Affections. The History of Redemption*, on the other hand, while it certainly can be regarded as a treatise, was cast by Edwards in the form of sermons that represent the sort of series Dwight mentions. The work, in fact, consists of thirty sermons on *one* text, Isaiah 51:8, 'For the moth shall eat them up like a garment . . .'. John Erskine, who first published the text in 1774, took it out of its sermonic form and made it read 'continuously' as a treatise. In the Yale edition, the work has been restored to its original form as a series of sermons: *A History of the Work of Redemption*, ed. John F. Wilson, *The Works of Jonathan Edwards* 9 (New Haven and London: Yale University Press, 1989). Wilson's Introduction is enormously helpful for an understanding of this work; see pp. 20ff. for the history of its publication.

4 Dwight has preserved the description of the occasion at Enfield given by the Rev. Dr Trumbull: 'When they went into the meeting house, the appearance of the assembly was thoughtless and vain. The people hardly conducted themselves with common decency. The Rev. Mr. Edwards of Northampton preached; and before the sermon was ended, the assembly appeared deeply impressed, and bowed down with an awful conviction of their sin and danger. There was such a breathing of distress and weeping, that the preacher was obliged to speak to the people and desire silence, that he might be heard' (Dwight, *Life*, p. 605).

5 Dwight, p. 604.

6 *Jonathan Edwards, Representative Selections*, ed. Clarence H. Faust and Thomas H. Johnson (New York: American Book Company, 1935), p. 145.

7 Ibid., pp. 138–9.

8 This sermon appears under two titles, 'God Glorified in Man's Dependence' and 'God Glorified in the Work of Redemption'. The difference stems from two ways of reducing the original full title—'God Glorified in the Work of Redemption, by the Greatness of Man's Dependence upon him, in the whole of it'.

9 Perry Miller, *Jonathan Edwards* (New York: William Sloane Associates, 1949), p. 30.

10 The 'Catalogue' has not as yet been fully transcribed and edited in the Yale edition, but the manuscript has been used by several editors in their work. See *Apocalyptic Writings*, ed. Stephen J. Stein, *The Works of Jonathan Edwards* 5 (New Haven and London: Yale University Press, 1977), pp. 54–74. Although Stein is concerned chiefly with Edwards's commentary on the Book of Revelation, Stein's use of the 'Catalogue' to show the many books Edwards had read in the Apocalyptic literature is indicative of both Edwards's vast learning and the value of the 'Catalogue' in providing information about the sources Edwards used. Revelation is the only book in the Bible to which Edwards devoted a separate commentary, but there is every reason to believe that the exacting scholarship exhibited in this work is typical of his treatment of Scripture as a whole. The 'Cata-

logue' is a quarto booklet of 24 leaves, paged by Edwards, 1–43. It contains a great variety of kinds of entries. There are notes of books to be looked for or to be bought, books read, comments on and condensations of books, quotations, instructions to himself, for example, a note to the effect that if a certain book is obtained, a portion of another book can be omitted as unnecessary. Some help in understanding the 'Catalogue' is found in the fact that many entries are correlated with the 'Miscellanies', with the sermons and the sermon notebooks.

11 See *Apocalyptic Writings*, p. 11. The list is taken from Edwards's 'Catalogue'.

12 This is the short title for a work Edwards wrote in 1747, *An Humble Attempt to Promote Explicit Agreement and Visible Union of God's People in Extraordinary Prayer*. The aim was to arrange a concert of prayer for the revival of religion between congregations in Scotland, England, New England and some other eastern states in America.

13 *Apocalyptic Writings*, p. 319. The form is the infinitive absolute.

14 *Apocalyptic Writings*, pp. 319–20.

Index

INDEX